Writing the Critical Essay

TERRORISM

An OPPOSING  VIEWPOINTS® Guide

Other books in the Writing the Critical Essay series:

Writing the Critical Essay

TERRORISM

An OPPOSING VIEWPOINTS® Guide

Stephen Currie, *Book Editor*

Bruce Glassman, *Vice President*
Bonnie Szumski, *Publisher, Series Editor*
Helen Cothran, *Managing Editor*

OPPOSING
VIEWPOINTS®
SERIES

GREENHAVEN PRESS
An imprint of Thomson Gale, a part of The Thomson Corporation

THOMSON
★
GALE

Detroit • New York • San Francisco • San Diego • New Haven, Conn. • Waterville, Maine • London • Munich

THOMSON

™

GALE

LIBRARY OF CONGRESS CATALOGING-IN-PUBLICATION DATA

Terrorism / Stephen Currie, book editor.
   p. cm. — (Writing the critical essay)
  Includes bibliographical references and index.
  ISBN 0-7377-3206-7 (lib. bdg. : alk. paper)
  1. Terrorism. 2. War on Terrorism, 2001–3. Terrorism—Government policy—United States. 4. Essay—Authorship. 5. Rhetoric. I. Currie, Stephen, 1960– II. Series.
  HV6431.T4577 2006
  363.32'0973—dc22

                                                    2005049314

Printed in the United States of America

CONTENTS

Section Two: Model Essays and Writing Exercises

Section Three: Supporting Research Material

Examining the state of writing and how it is taught in the United States was the official purpose of the National Commission on Writing in America's Schools and Colleges. The commission, made up of teachers, school administrators, business leaders, and college and university presidents, released its first report in 2003. "Despite the best efforts of many educators," commissioners argued, "writing has not received the full attention it deserves." Among the findings of the commission was that most fourth-grade students spent less than three hours a week writing, that three-quarters of high school seniors never receive a writing assignment in their history or social studies classes, and that more than 50 percent of first-year students in college have problems writing error-free papers. The commission called for a "cultural sea change" that would increase the emphasis on writing for both elementary and secondary schools. These conclusions have made some educators realize that writing must be emphasized in the curriculum. As colleges are demanding an ever-higher level of writing proficiency from incoming students, schools must respond by making students more competent writers. In response to these concerns, the SAT, an influential standardized test used for college admissions, required an essay for the first time in 2005.

Books in the Writing the Critical Essay: An Opposing Viewpoints Guide series use the patented Opposing Viewpoints format to help students learn to organize ideas and arguments and to write essays using common critical writing techniques. Each book in the series focuses on a particular type of essay writing—including expository, persuasive, descriptive, and narrative—that students learn while being taught both the five-paragraph essay as well as longer pieces of writing that have an opinionated focus. These guides include everything necessary to help students research, outline, draft, edit, and ultimately write successful essays across the curriculum, including essays for the SAT.

Using Opposing Viewpoints

This series is inspired by and builds upon Greenhaven Press's acclaimed Opposing Viewpoints series. As in the parent series, each book in the Writing the Critical Essay series focuses on a timely and controversial social issue that provides lots of opportunities for creating thought-provoking essays. The first section of each volume begins with a brief introductory essay that provides context for the opposing viewpoints that follow. These articles are chosen for their accessibility and clearly stated views. The thesis of each article is made explicit in the article's title and is accentuated by its pairing with an opposing or alternative view. These essays are both models of persuasive writing techniques and valuable research material that students can mine to write their own informed essays. Guided reading and discussion questions help lead students to key ideas and writing techniques presented in the selections.

The second section of each book begins with a preface discussing the format of the essays and examining characteristics of the featured essay type. Model five-paragraph and longer essays then demonstrate that essay type. The essays are annotated so that key writing elements and techniques are pointed out to the student. Sequential, step-by-step exercises help students construct and refine thesis statements; organize material into outlines; analyze and try out writing techniques; write transitions, introductions, and conclusions; and incorporate quotations and other researched material. Ultimately, students construct their own compositions using the designated essay type.

The third section of each volume provides additional research material and writing prompts to help the student. Additional facts about the topic of the book serve as a convenient source of supporting material for essays. Other features help students go beyond the book for their research. Like other Greenhaven Press books, each book in the Writing the Critical Essay series includes bibliographic listings of relevant periodical articles, books, Web sites, and organizations to contact.

Writing the Critical Essay: An Opposing Viewpoints Guide will help students master essay techniques that can be used in any discipline.

Background to Controversy: The Problem of Terrorism

On September 11, 2001, four American passenger airplanes were hijacked soon after taking off from East Coast airports. The hijackers were members of a group called al Qaeda, a Muslim terrorist organization dedicated to using violence and fear to attack the foundations of Western society. The terrorists steered two of the airplanes directly into the Twin Towers of the World Trade Center in New York and a third into the Pentagon complex just outside Washington, D.C. The fourth airplane crashed in a Pennsylvania field when passengers stormed the cockpit to take the controls from the hijackers; one al Qaeda leader has claimed that it was heading for the U.S. Capitol. Nearly three thousand people were killed in the attacks, making the disaster the single deadliest event on American soil since the Battle of Antietam during the Civil War.

Although there had been other terrorist attacks before September 11, the events of that day had an impact that went far beyond any previous attacks. The al Qaeda attacks were dramatic, vicious, and extremely deadly. Moreover, the attacks were the work of a large, wealthy, and well-organized group of terrorists. In the wake of September 11, many Americans realized for the first time the power of America's enemies—and the intensity of their hatred for the United States. In one stroke, September 11 changed the way Americans thought about the world around them and their own safety as a nation. The tragedies of that day forced Americans to acknowledge their own vulnerability to attack. The world would never seem quite so secure again.

Terrorists and Terrorist Groups

The American reaction to September 11 was exactly what al Qaeda forces had hoped to achieve. The goal of terrorism is

The September 11, 2001, attacks on the World Trade Center marked the beginning of a new age of antiterrorism in the United States.

in part to destroy and to kill, but it is also to inspire terror—to make ordinary people live in fear. To this end, terrorist groups typically strike quickly and without warning. They are not a part of any national government. Indeed, unlike soldiers affiliated with national armies, terrorists spend much of their time in hiding. They communicate secretly, and they routinely change their bases of operations. And instead of attacking ordinary military targets, such as soldiers on a battlefield, terrorists typically aim for innocent civilians.

These realities make terrorism difficult to fight. Because terrorist organizations are so secretive, outsiders have no easy way of knowing who is—and who is not—a member. It is hard to locate terrorist groups, and hard to destroy them if they are found. Terrorists do not formally declare war, nor do they usually telegraph their intentions in other ways. Certainly, before September 11, 2001, few U.S. officials suspected that terrorists might turn passenger airplanes into lethal suicide bombs. Unpredictability, in short, is the hallmark of terrorism.

Despite the difficulties of battling terrorism, the American government knew it had to respond to the September 11 attacks. It did so by initiating a two-pronged effort known as the war on terror. One important part of this effort has involved the use of military force. American intelligence operatives believed that many al Qaeda operatives were hiding in Afghanistan, a country with a government friendly to the organization and sympathetic to its aims. As a result, President George W. Bush launched a military attack on Afghanistan in late 2001. American forces quickly deposed Afghanistan's government and captured several al Qaeda leaders—though as of July 2005 the whereabouts of the group's founder, Osama bin Laden, remain unknown.

U.S. fighter pilots conduct a combat mission over Afghanistan in April 2002.

Bush soon shifted his focus from Afghanistan to Iraq, a Middle Eastern country run at the time by dictator Saddam Hussein. Bush asserted that there were close ties between

Hussein's regime and al Qaeda officials. He also argued that Iraq was hoarding dangerous weapons that might make their way into the hands of terrorists. With the support of Congress and some other nations, notably Great Britain, the United States attacked Iraq in 2003. As in Afghanistan, U.S. troops quickly destroyed the old regime and began the arduous process of building a new government.

These military actions, however, proved controversial. Some Americans fear that massive displays of force may anger and alienate people around the world, especially in the Middle East. Others claim that the war in Iraq, in particular, was fought on false pretenses. As of 2005, they point out, no definitive connection between Hussein and al Qaeda has been found, and the search for Hussein's supposed weapon stockpiles has revealed nothing. Critics of military action charge that the wars have inflamed tensions and increased resentment of the United States, without making the world safer from terrorist attacks. Indeed, some argue, the military response has unwittingly increased the appeal of terrorist groups in the Middle East and elsewhere.

New Security Measures

The second prong of the war on terror involves preventing terrorism on a domestic level. This effort includes a wide variety of measures and tactics. Government officials, for example, have tightened airline security, banning such items as nail clippers and jackknives from carry-on baggage and requiring passengers to present identification before they board a plane. Following September 11, too, public access to important government buildings such as the Capitol and the White House has been severely limited. On a larger scale, President Bush has established a new Department of Homeland Security, charged with coordinating antiterrorism efforts among various government agencies.

A few of these measures have been controversial. In its fight against terrorist activities, the government has

assumed powers it has usually been denied in the past. Under certain circumstances, for instance, the government may hold suspected terrorists for long periods of time without formally charging them or allowing them to consult with a lawyer. Similarly, under the Patriot Act—a set of laws passed soon after the September 11 disaster—government officials can access certain otherwise private records of ordinary citizens suspected of being terrorists or of working with terrorist groups. Some Americans believe that these laws increase public safety. Others, however, argue that the Patriot Act and similar measures infringe on the basic freedoms of Americans.

A soldier and a specially trained dog search a warehouse for explosive devices.

Fears and Realities

Despite a lack of terrorism on American soil since 2001, the fear of terrorism remains great in post–September 11 America. News articles discuss the capture and questioning of suspected terrorists at border crossings. Homeland Security officials assess the risks of terrorist activity each

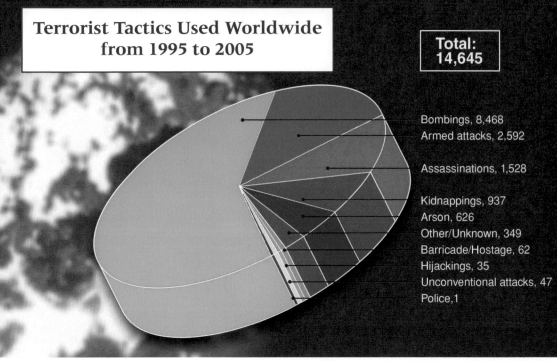

Terrorist Tactics Used Worldwide from 1995 to 2005

Total: 14,645

Bombings, 8,468
Armed attacks, 2,592

Assassinations, 1,528

Kidnappings, 937
Arson, 626
Other/Unknown, 349
Barricade/Hostage, 62
Hijackings, 35
Unconventional attacks, 47
Police,1

Source: Information from the Terrorism Knowledge Database, www.tkb.org, May 25, 2005. Supported by the National Memorial Institute for the Prevention of Terrorism (MIPT).

day and issue alerts to the public based on their estimation of the danger. Television specials discuss the vulnerability of America's tunnels and bridges to terrorist attack or caution that the government is not doing enough to search the contents of cargo ships arriving in American ports. The overwhelming majority of Americans have never been directly affected by a terrorist attack—yet many, many people in the United States nonetheless worry about when, and where, the next attack will strike.

The reality is that no governmental measures can completely prevent the possibility of terrorist attacks. Whether through threats or direct action, a terrorist who is completely devoted to inflicting damage to America will succeed in creating havoc and fear. The debate over terrorism in modern America, then, is not about whether terrorism can be stopped. Rather, the debate is about the level of the threat, the effectiveness of the responses to that threat, and the pros and cons of putting those responses into place. The problem of terrorism is one of the most serious of modern times, and these questions will not be settled easily.

Section One:
Opposing
Viewpoints
on Terrorism

The War in Iraq Has Reduced the Threat of Terrorism

Douglas J. Feith

Douglas J. Feith served in President George W. Bush's administration as Undersecretary of Defense for Policy. In this position, he was responsible for helping to determine U.S. military strategy. Feith argues in this excerpt that American success in Iraq will strike a major blow at terrorism in the Middle East and elsewhere.

Consider the following questions:

1. According to Feith, what are the three main elements of the U.S. response to terrorism?
2. What does Feith mean when he says that U.S. efforts have forced terrorists to "shift . . . from offense to defense"?
3. According to President Bush, why is it important to create a democratic government in Iraq?

How can we fight a global war against enemies who are present in so many countries with whom we are not at war?

A key part of the answer is cooperation with partner countries. As a practical matter in most cases, only they can act as required against the terrorists on their territory. The required action may be law enforcement; it may be intelligence work; it may be a military operation; or it may be the development of an educational system that can compete with extremist madrassa schools [a type of Islamic educational institution].

Douglas J. Feith, "Freedom, Safety, and Sovereignty," www.pentagon.com, February 17, 2005.

We're working with allies and partners to develop common views on the nature of the threat of terrorist extremism. We're assessing with them the capabilities needed to confront it. We urge our partners to do their duty as sovereign states to regulate their borders and otherwise control their territories.

And we're working to build their capacity to perform that duty. So the United States not only encourages partner action, but helps to enable it. This accounts for such various, not obviously related projects as:

- the training and equipping of the Afghan and Iraqi security forces, military and police;
- counter-terrorist train-and-equip efforts in Pakistan, Yemen, the Philippines, Georgia and elsewhere;
- educational assistance programs in various countries;

The creation of Iraqi military forces, such as these soldiers-in-training, has been a large part of the rebuilding process in Iraq.

- The President's Global Peace Operations Initiative, to help train, sustain and rapidly deploy forces (initially mainly in Africa) for peacekeeping and for the more difficult missions known as "peace enforcement"; and
- the establishment of the new Reconstruction and Stabilization Office at the State Department to help countries develop the tools they need for civil administration.

The main elements of U.S. strategy in the war on terrorism are: one, protecting the homeland; two, disrupting and attacking terrorist networks; and three, countering ideological support for terrorism. The third—the ideological fight—we see as the key to victory.

Former Iraqi leader Saddam Hussein is shown here after his capture in 2003.

We have overthrown two regimes that supported terrorists—that of the Taliban in Afghanistan and of Saddam Hussein in Iraq—and induced a third—[Muammar] Qaddafi's in Libya—to change its policies. All of this has contributed to forcing our extremist enemies to shift some of their attention from offense to defense. All of this has helped interfere with their communications, planning, weapons programs, training and operations, as have our disruptions of terrorist financial flows and the capture or killing of approximately two-thirds of the known leadership of al Qaida. But we recognize that, if all we do is disrupt and attack terrorist networks, we'll not defeat our enemies.

Our goal is not only to deny the terrorists what they need to operate, but ultimately to deny them what they need to survive. This is why it is crucial to counter ideological support for terrorism.

In January 2005 an Iraqi woman living in Jordan casts an absentee ballot in Iraq's first democratic election in five decades.

As we see it, this effort, a long-term undertaking, has two components. First, we have to de-legitimate terrorism. As the President has said, we intend to make terrorism like the slave trade, piracy, or genocide—activities that nobody who aspires to respectability can condone, much less support. It will take a lot of work to change the way millions of people think, and to undo the effects of decades in which terrorism was tolerated and even, on occasion, rewarded.

The second component of our effort to counter ideological support for terrorism is support for models of moderation, democracy, sound economics and healthy civil society that can compete with the bloody blandishments of the extremists. As President Bush, referring to the Greater Middle East, has explained, "As long as that region is a place of tyranny and despair and anger, it will produce men and movements that threaten the safety of Americans and our friends. We seek the advance of democracy for the most practical of reasons: because democracies do not support terrorists or threaten the world with weapons of mass murder." This is why the political and economic reconstruction of Afghanistan and Iraq are crucial to success in the war on terrorism.

Analyze the essay:

1. What claim does Feith make about former Iraqi dictator Saddam Hussein? How does this claim support Feith's thesis?
2. In his commentary, Feith links U.S. military efforts in Iraq with American projects, military and otherwise, in other countries. What point is he trying to make by bringing up these connections?
3. Is Feith's argument strengthened or weakened by the fact that he works for the Department of Defense? Why?

The War in Iraq Has Increased the Threat of Terrorism

Bob Herbert

Bob Herbert, a columnist for the *New York Times,* argues in this excerpt that the war in Iraq has made the threat of a U.S. terror attack worse. Herbert asserts that the war in Iraq has been at best a distraction from the war on terrorism. In his view, the war has energized jihadists, radical Islamic terrorists convinced that they are fighting a holy war against America, and encouraged anti-American feelings.

Consider the following questions:

1. According to Herbert, what warnings was President Bush given before going to war? In Herbert's view, have later events justified those warnings? Why or why not?
2. In Herbert's opinion, where should the United States be focusing its resources?
3. According to Herbert, how has the Bush administration perverted the ideals of freedom and democracy while waging war against Iraq?

I remember going to Washington in mid-March 2003, nearly two years ago, to cover a demonstration by tens of thousands of protesters who were clinging to the last, tissue-thin strands of hope that they could bring the Bush administration to its senses and prevent the invasion of Iraq.

But it was already clear that nothing would deter President Bush from his war. I filed a column that said, "We're about to watch the tragedy unfold."

Bob Herbert, "Iraq, Then and Now," *New York Times,* February 21, 2005. Copyright © 2005 by The New York Times Company. Reproduced by permission.

Even more clearly than the protests that weekend, I remember the ominous stories in the press about the likelihood that a war in Iraq would embolden Islamic terrorist organizations and strengthen their recruitment efforts. The [New York] Times ran a front-page article on Sunday March 16 [2003], in which a senior counterintelligence official said: "An American invasion of Iraq is already being used as a recruitment tool by Al Qaeda and other groups. And it is a very effective tool."

On the same day the Washington Post reported that "specialists inside and outside the government question whether a U.S.-led invasion of Iraq would deliver a significant blow against international terrorism. Experts warn that war and occupation could also have the opposite effect by emboldening radical Islamic groups and adding to their grievances."

U.S. soldiers arrest a group of men in Baghdad accused of ambushing coalition troops.

All warnings were given the back of the administration's hand. Mr. Bush launched his invasion and many thousands died. Now fast-forward to last week's [February 2005] testimony of top administration officials before the Senate Intelligence Committee. If the war in Iraq was supposed to stem the terrorist tide, the comments of these officials made it clear that it hasn't worked.

Porter Goss, the C.I.A. director, told the committee, "Islamic extremists are exploiting the Iraqi conflict to recruit new anti-U.S, jihadists." He added, "These jihadists who survive will leave Iraq experienced and focus on acts of urban terrorism."

U.S. Soldier Casualties in Iraq

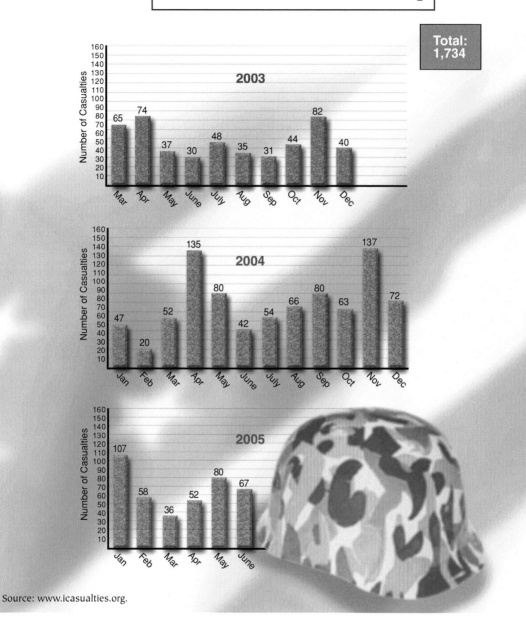

Total: 1,734

2003

Month	Number of Casualties
Mar	65
Apr	74
May	37
June	30
July	48
Aug	35
Sep	31
Oct	44
Nov	82
Dec	40

2004

Month	Number of Casualties
Jan	47
Feb	20
Mar	52
Apr	135
May	80
June	42
July	54
Aug	66
Sep	80
Oct	63
Nov	137
Dec	72

2005

Month	Number of Casualties
Jan	107
Feb	58
Mar	36
Apr	52
May	80
June	67

Source: www.icasualties.org.

The war, said Mr. Goss, "has become a cause for extremists." In his view, "It may only be a matter of time before Al Qaeda or another group attempts to use chemical, biological, radiological and nuclear weapons."

Vice Adm. Lowell Jacoby, director of the Defense Intelligence Agency, said: "Our policies in the Middle East fuel Islamic resentment. Overwhelming majorities in Morocco, Jordan and Saudi Arabia believe the U.S. has a negative policy toward the Arab world."

An article in last Friday's *Washington Post* said the radical group Ansar al-Islam, which has carried out dozens of suicide bombings in Iraq, is recruiting young Muslims across Europe to join the insurgency.

So tell me again. What was this war about? In terms of the fight against terror, the war in Iraq has been a big loss. We've energized the enemy. We've wasted the talents of the many men and women who have fought bravely and tenaciously in Iraq. Thousands upon thousands of American men and women have lost arms or legs, or been paralyzed

Pictured here are the ruins of a double-decker bus in London that was bombed by an eighteen-year-old Muslim suicide bomber on July 7, 2005.

A group of marines evacuates a wounded soldier. U.S. soldier casualties have continued to mount despite the end of major combat operations.

or blinded or horribly burned or killed in this ill-advised war. A wiser administration would have avoided that carnage and marshaled instead a more robust effort against Al Qaeda, which remains a deadly threat to America.

What is also dismaying is the way in which the administration has taken every opportunity since Sept. 11, 2001, to utilize the lofty language of freedom, democracy and the rule of law while secretly pursuing policies that are both unjust and profoundly inhumane. It is the policy of the U.S. to deny due process of law to detainees at the scandalous interrogation camp at Guantanamo Bay, Cuba, where prisoners, many of whom have turned out to be innocent, are routinely treated in a cruel and degrading manner.

The U.S. is also engaged in the reprehensible practice known as extraordinary rendition, in which terror suspects are abducted and sent off to be interrogated by foreign regimes that are known to practice torture. And the C.I.A. is operating ultrasecret prisons or detention centers overseas for so-called high-value detainees. What goes on in those places is anybody's guess.

It may be that most Americans would prefer not to know about these practices, which are nothing less than malignant cells that are already spreading in the nation's soul. Denial is often the first response to the most painful realities. But most Americans also know what happens when a cancer is ignored.

Analyze the essay:

1. Herbert writes that "nothing would deter President Bush from his war." Why do you think he used the phrase "his war"? What effect might that phrase have on the reader?
2. Which experts does Herbert quote to support his argument? Why did he choose these sources? How do they help strengthen his thesis?
3. What is Herbert's opinion of the men and women who are fighting in Iraq? Why do you think he gives this opinion?

The War on Terror Should Focus on Islamic Radicals

Cal Thomas

Political columnist Cal Thomas argues in this essay that the bulk of terrorists are Islamic radicals and that these terrorists present a great threat to the United States. Thomas criticizes the government and the media for ignoring the religious motivation of many of these terrorists. In his view, the war on terror should be defined as a war against Muslim extremism. Thomas argues that to do otherwise is shortsighted and foolish. This article was written in 2004, shortly after a terrorist attack in Beslan, Russia.

Consider the following questions:

1. According to Thomas, what course of action should moderate Muslims take in regard to terrorism? Why?
2. What does Muslim scholar Ali Abdullah say about the massacre in Beslan? What does Thomas think of Abdullah's comments?
3. What does Thomas mean by "political correctness"? How would he like American reporters and government officials to refer to Muslim terrorists?

Following the massacre by mostly Muslim terrorists in Beslan, Russia, that killed, at last count, 338 people, including at least 156 children, and wounded hundreds of others, a rare voice of reason was heard from an unlikely place.

Cal Thomas, "State of the War on Terrorism: Political Correctness on Terrorism Must End," *Beaumont Enterprise*, September 12, 2004. Copyright © 2004 by Tribune Media Services, Inc. All rights reserved. Reproduced by permission.

Abdulrahman al-Rashed, general manager of Al-Arabiya television in Dubai, wrote in a London Arabic newspaper, *Asharq Al-Awsat*, "Our terrorist sons are an end-product of our corrupted culture."

Under the headline "The Painful Truth: All the World Terrorists Are Muslims!," he wrote, "Most perpetrators of suicide operations in buses, schools and residential buildings around the world for the past 10 years have been Muslims." He also wrote that if Muslims want to change their image, they must "admit the scandalous facts," rather than disparage critics or justify terrorists' behavior.

As a good Baptist would say, "Amen!" It's about time somebody spoke the truth. From Russia to Iraq, from the Sudan to the Philippines, and from Madrid, Bali and Kenya to the World Trade Center in New York, a field in Pennsylvania and the Pentagon in Washington, one characteristic describes all of the killers: They are Muslims.

Russian police apprehend one of the attackers in the 2004 Beslan school massacre that killed more than three hundred people.

In the Russian killings, the news agency Itar-Tass reports that at least 10 of the 32 hostage terrorists were linked to al-Qaida or had ties to Arab nations. Despite these facts, major American media are going out of their way to cover up the obvious, preferring words such as "militants" and "extremists," and refusing in many cases to identify the religious motivation behind the killings.

The U.S. government is promoting "tolerance" and "diversity" sessions led by Muslim organizations, some of which have questionable ties to groups that have either supported or condemned with disingenuous statements killings by Muslim extremists, or sought to justify them because of policies promoted by Israel or the United States.

Repeatedly, these mandatory sessions tell government employees that Islam is a peaceful religion from which they have nothing to fear. If that is so, why aren't the "moderates" leading an army of their own and crushing the "infidels" who have supposedly "hijacked" this "peaceful religion"?

"Moderate" Islamic clerics should defrock and denounce other clerics who preach hate and the destruction of Christians, Jews and all things Western. These diversity

Gorrell. © 2002 by Creators Syndicate, Inc. Reproduced by permission of Bob Gorrell.

The Muslim cleric Muhammad Metin Kaplan wants to create a worldwide Islamic state. Its goal would involve the destruction of Western civilization.

and sensitivity sessions should be held in countries that harbor and train terrorists and export terrorism as a religious mandate and a national policy.

Instead, we hear from Ali Abdullah, an Islamic scholar in Bahrain, who said of the massacre in Russia: "I have no doubt that this is the work of the Israelis who want to tarnish the image of Muslims and are working alongside Russians who have their own agenda against the Muslims in Chechnya [a part of Russia where civil war has raged for many years]." Omar Bakri Mohammed, the leader of the extremist sect al-Muhajiroun, told London's *Sunday Telegraph,* "If an Iraqi Muslim carried out an attack like (the Russian massacre) in Britain, it would be justified because Britain has carried out acts of terrorism in Iraq."

It gives a whole new meaning to "women and children first." Mohammed's interview was in conjunction with a "celebratory" conference in London this weekend to commemorate the third anniversary of the Sept. 11 attacks on the United States.

It's long past time to ditch political correctness and identify the enemy, which is not disembodied "terrorism" but radical Islamists who commit terror in the perverted name of their god.

A report from The Institute of World Politics in Washington claims that Saudi Arabia has spent tens of millions of dollars on indoctrinating American soldiers and prison inmates in radical Islamic ideology and that its goal is to create insurgency cells in the United States devoted to the Wahhabi [a Muslim sect] agenda.

The Muslim vote may go to John Kerry this time [the 2004 presidential election] (it mostly went for President Bush in 2000) because Kerry is perceived by some Muslim leaders as potentially more sympathetic to their objective of ending support for Israel and eliminating the Patriot Act, which has kept an eye on people and places known for Islamic extremist behavior and potential jihadists who want to kill us.

We should be listening to Abdulrahman al-Rashed or, for a reality check, former Malaysian Prime Minister Mahathir Mohamad, who last October called on the world's 1.3 billion Muslims to unite against "a few million Jews," whom he said rule the world and get others to fight and die for them.

Moderate? Peaceful? Where is the evidence?

Analyze the essay:

1. What is Thomas's view of Islam in general? What evidence in the article leads you to this conclusion? How does Thomas's view of Islam support or weaken his argument?
2. How would you characterize the tone of Thomas's essay? What words and phrases does he use to make his point? Do his tone and choice of words make his argument more or less convincing? Why?

The War on Terror Should Focus on U.S. Radicals

Nicholas D. Kristof

Nicholas D. Kristof is a commentator for the *New York Times*. In this column, Kristof argues that certain American hate groups, such as white supremacist organizations, threaten the security of the United States. While acknowledging the dangers posed by Islamic groups such as al Qaeda, Kristof asserts that American officials do not pay enough attention to homegrown terrorism. This column was written shortly after the fatal shootings of the husband and mother of Joan Humphrey Lefkow, a federal judge who had received death threats from a member of one of these groups.

Consider the following questions:

1. Who is Matt Hale? What are his beliefs? What is Kristof's opinion of Hale's beliefs?
2. What evidence does Kristof provide to back up his assertion that white supremacist groups are dangerous?
3. In Kristof's view, how did the September 11 attacks change the way law enforcement officials dealt with American hate groups?

Before the "Rev. Dr." Matt Hale, the white racist leader, was arrested for seeking the murder of a federal judge, and long before the judge returned home last week to find her husband and mother murdered, I had lunch with him.

Nicholas D. Kristof, "Homegrown Osamas," *New York Times*, March 9, 2005.

The FBI is offering a reward up to $50,000 for information leading to the identification and arrest of individual(s) responsible for the mur of Michael Lefkow and Donna Humphrey.

On 02/28/2005, Michael Lefkow and Donna Humphrey were murdered in their residence in the vicinity of the 5200 block of North Lakewood Ave., Chicago, IL.

If you have any information regarding these homicides, please the joint Chicago Police Department / FBI Task Force Chicago or (312) 744-5000 if outside of Chicago

The FBI offers a reward for information leading to the arrest of those responsible for the murders of relatives of Federal District Judge Joan Humphrey Lefkow.

Mr. Hale, who is smart, articulate and malignant, ranted about "race betrayers" as he picked at his fruit salad: "Interracial marriage is against nature. . . ."

"Oh?" I replied. "Incidentally, my wife is Chinese-American."

There was an awkward silence.

Mr. Hale was convicted last year of soliciting the murder of Federal District Judge Joan Humphrey Lefkow. Now the police are investigating whether there is any link between Mr. Hale or his followers and the murders. Some white supremacists celebrated the killings, but Mr. Hale has strongly denied any involvement.

The possibility that extremists carried out the murders for revenge or intimidation sends a chill through our judicial system, because it would then constitute an assault on our judiciary itself. Throughout U.S. history, only three federal judges have been murdered, but all three murders occurred after 1978 and all at their homes.

Threats to federal judges and prosecutors have increased sharply since they began to be tabulated 25 years ago, but the attack on Judge Lefkow's family, if it was related to her work, would take such threats to a new level. Who would want to be a judge if that risked the lives of loved ones?

Whatever the circumstances of those murders, Mr. Hale provides a scary window into a niche of America that few of us know much about. Since 9/11, we've focused almost exclusively on the risk of terrorism from Muslim foreigners, but we have plenty of potential homegrown Osamas.

I interviewed Mr. Hale in 2002 because I had heard that he was becoming a key figure in America's hate community, recruiting followers with a savvy high-tech marketing machine. Over lunch in East Peoria, Ill., he described how as a schoolboy he had become a racist after seeing white girls kissing black boys.

"I felt nauseous," he told me earnestly.

Mr. Hale said attacks on race-betrayers and "mud people" [a phrase used by Hale to describe people other than white Christians] were understandable but a waste of time. "Suppose someone goes out and kills 10 blacks tonight," he said, shrugging. "Well, there are millions more."

What troubled me most about Mr. Hale was not his extremist views, but his obvious organizational ability and talent to inspire his followers. When he was denied a law

Matt Hale holds up a letter from one of his followers. Hale was denied a license to practice law in the state of Illinois because of his extremist views.

Texan William Krar is escorted to prison in 2004 after being sentenced to more than eleven years for stockpiling an arsenal of illegal weapons.

license in 1999 because of his racist views, a follower went on a rampage and shot 11 people—all blacks, Asians or Jews.

After the Oklahoma City bombing [in which white supremacist Timothy McVeigh blew up a federal building in 1995], American law enforcement authorities cracked down quite effectively on domestic racists and militia leaders. But Mark Potok of the Southern Poverty Law Center, which monitors 760 hate groups with about 100,000 members, notes that after 9/11, the law enforcement focus switched overwhelmingly to [cracking down on] Arabs.

The Feds are right to be especially alarmed about Al Qaeda. But we also need to be more vigilant about the domestic white supremacists, neo-Nazis and militia members. After all, some have more W.M.D. [weapons of mass destruction] than Saddam [Hussein].

Two years ago, for example, a Texan in a militia, William Krar, was caught with 25 machine guns and other weapons, a quarter-million rounds of ammunition, 60 pipe bombs and enough sodium cyanide to kill hundreds of people.

We were too complacent about Al Qaeda and foreign terrorists before 9/11. And now we're too complacent about homegrown threats.

Mr. Hale handed me some of his church's gospels, including "The White Man's Bible"—which embarrassed me at the airport when I was selected for a random security screening and the contents of my bag laid out on a table. Then, even though the screeners apparently believed that I was a neo-Nazi with violent, racist tracts, they let me board without any further check.

That "White Man's Bible" says: "We don't need the Jews, the [blacks], or any other mud people. We have the fighting creed to re-affirm the White Man's triumph of the will as heroically demonstrated by that greatest of all White leaders—Adolf Hitler. So let us get into the fight today, now! You have no alibi, no other way out, White Man! It's either Fight or Die!"

So we don't have to go to Saudi Arabia to find violent religious extremists steeped in hatred for all America stands for. Wake up—they're here.

Analyze the essay:

1. What emotions does Kristof hope to arouse in the reader by quoting Hale's own words? How do these words indirectly help support Kristof's thesis?

2. In what ways, according to Kristof, are Hale and his followers "homegrown Osamas"? What parallels does he draw between Hale and radical Islamic terrorists to make his point?

Americans Should Fear a Terrorist Attack

Stephen Flynn

Stephen Flynn has served in several posts in the military and in the U.S. government and was the lead author of a government report entitled "America: Still Unprepared, Still in Danger." The report, like Flynn's book *America the Vulnerable,* argues that the U.S. government has not taken appropriate action to stop terrorist attacks. Flynn is concerned that a terrorist strike is likely to happen and that the United States is poorly prepared for this possibility. The excerpt below explains Flynn's thinking.

Consider the following questions:

1. According to Flynn, how is today's war on terrorism different from American wars and conflicts of the past?
2. How does Flynn characterize the average American's fears of terrorism? Would he say most Americans are overly fearful of attack, or not nearly fearful enough? Why?
3. According to the author, what can the United States do to defuse anti-American sentiment in the world? What does Flynn see as the limits to this approach?

I f September 11, 2001, was a wake-up call, clearly America has fallen back asleep. Our return to complacency could not be more foolhardy. The 9/11 attacks were not an aberration. The same forces that helped to produce the hor-

Stephen Flynn, *America the Vulnerable: How Our Government Is Failing to Protect Us from Terrorism.* New York: HarperCollins, 2004. Copyright © 2004 by HarperCollins Publishers Inc. Reproduced by permission.

Despite increased security measures, America's bridges and subways remain largely unprotected from terrorist attack.

ror that befell the nation on that day continue to gather strength. Yet we appear to be unwilling to do what must be done to make our society less of a target. Instead, we are sailing into a national security version of the Perfect Storm [that is, disaster].

Homeland security has entered our post–9/11 lexicon, but homeland insecurity remains the abiding reality. With

South Korean demonstrators burn an American flag in 2002.

the exception of airports, much of what is critical to our way of life remains unprotected. Despite all the rhetoric, after the initial flurry of activity to harden cockpit doors and confiscate nail clippers, there has been little appetite in Washington to move beyond government reorganization and color-coded alerts. While we receive a steady diet of somber warnings about potential terrorist attacks, the new federal outlays for homeland security in the two years after 9/11 command an investment equal to only 4 percent of the Pentagon's annual budget. Outside of Washington, pink slips for police officers and firefighters are more common than new public investments in security. With state and local budgets hemorrhaging red ink, mayors, county commissioners, and governors are simply in no position to fill the security void the federal government has been keen to thrust upon them. The private sector has shown its preference for taking a minimalist approach to new security responsibilities. There have been private-sector leaders who have been bucking this trend. . . . But, by and large, trade and industry associations have been hard at work trying to fend off new security requirements that might compel them to address vulnerabilities and thereby raise their bottom-line costs.

From water and food supplies; refineries, energy grids, and pipelines; bridges, tunnels, trains, trucks, and cargo containers; to the cyber backbone that underpins the information age in which we live, the measures we have been cobbling together are hardly fit to deter amateur thieves, vandals, and hackers, never mind determined terrorists. Worse still, small improvements are often oversold as giant steps forward, lowering the guard of average citizens as they carry on their daily routine with an unwarranted sense of confidence.

Old habits die hard. The truth is America has been on a hundred-year joyride. Throughout the twentieth century we were able to treat national security as essentially an out-of-body experience. When confronted by threats, we dealt with them on the turf of our allies or our adversaries. Aside from the occasional disaster and

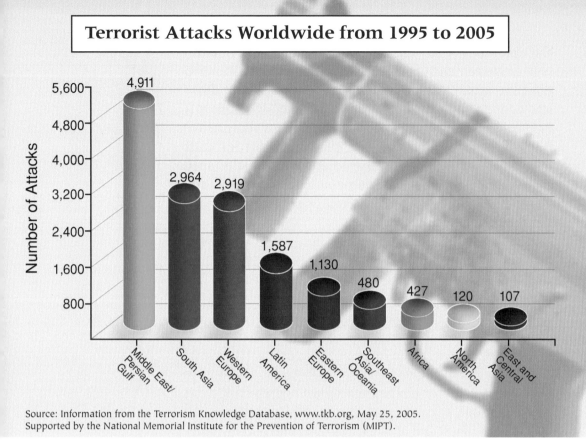

Terrorist Attacks Worldwide from 1995 to 2005

Number of Attacks

- Middle East/Persian Gulf: 4,911
- South Asia: 2,964
- Western Europe: 2,919
- Latin America: 1,587
- Eastern Europe: 1,130
- Southeast Asia/Oceania: 480
- Africa: 427
- North America: 120
- East and Central Asia: 107

Source: Information from the Terrorism Knowledge Database, www.tkb.org, May 25, 2005.
Supported by the National Memorial Institute for the Prevention of Terrorism (MIPT).

heinous crime, civilian life at home has been virtually terror-free. Then, out of the blue, the 9/11 attacks turned our national security world on its head. Al Qaeda exposed our Achilles' heel. Paradoxically, the United States has no rival when it comes to projecting its military, economic, and cultural power around the world. But we are practically defenseless at home.

A number of post–Cold War realities have created a new global environment that places America in a position of especially grave danger. First, from nearly all points on the compass, there is rising anti-Americanism. To a large extent this is the inevitable by-product of the United States' unique standing as the sole remaining superpower. Our current predicament is that any unhappy person on the planet is inclined to lay the blame on America's doorstep. If they think their society is being undermined by cultural pollution, they are likely to see the United

States as the lead polluter. If they view the economic rules of the game as rigged to benefit the few at the cost of the many, they castigate the United States as the capitalist kingmaker. And if they imagine life would be better if there were a change in the local political landscape, they see the United States as standing in the background, or foreground, as a barrier to their revisionist dreams. When our actions and policies display periodic arrogance and indifference, we only add grist to the anti-U.S. mill.

For the foreseeable future, increased anti-Americanism will be a fact of life. Certainly it can be exacerbated or ameliorated by the approaches we take and the priority we assign to addressing some of the world's most pressing public-policy challenges. There is too much pent-up rage and frustration around the world caused by overpopulation, limited education and job opportunities, and a lack of participation in the political process. As a nation, we should be mindful of these sobering realities and work to improve them wherever we can. But even the wisest, kindest, and gentlest American leadership will not appease groups like the remnants of the Taliban, whose beliefs are the antithesis of our own. There will be ample recruits to strike out at the United States as a means of defending or advancing their causes.

> ## Terrorist Attacks Are Inevitable
>
> **It's not a matter of if, just a matter of when, in terms of terrorist attacks.**
>
> Los Angeles police chief William Bratton, quoted in Tom Costello, "Four Years After 9/11, U.S. Transit Still at Risk," *MSNBC.com*, July 7, 2005.

This rise in discontent is made more menacing by another disturbing fact of twenty-first-century life: groups with no governmental ties can acquire the most lethal tools of warfare. Certainly, state sponsorship can be helpful. But with so many pockets of the world hosting open-air arms bazaars, complicity with an established government is not essential. At one end of the spectrum, weapons like the AK-47 are so plentiful that they can be had for the price of a chicken in Uganda, the price of a goat in Kenya, and the price of a bag of maize in Mozambique or Angola. At the other end, there is enough separated plutonium and highly enriched uranium in the world to make thousands of nuclear weapons. Weapons-usable nuclear materials exist in over 130 research laboratories operating in more than forty countries around the world, ranging from Ukraine to Ghana.

Added to the growing motive and means to strike out at the United States, there is also enhanced opportunity in our interconnected global environment for criminals and terrorists to acquire wider reach. Over the past decade, drug smugglers, human traffickers, and gunrunners have found fewer barriers to their nefarious activities. As the worldwide networks that support international trade and travel become more open and the level of cross-border activities increase, the bad have benefited alongside the good.

Analyze the essay:

1. In his narrative Flynn hopes to make the reader recognize the dangers of terrorist attack. What words, phrases, and descriptions in the text illustrate and encourage these feelings of worry and fear? How do these advance Flynn's argument?

2. Flynn argues that the realities of the world in the twenty-first century have made the United States far more vulnerable to terrorism than ever before. What arguments does he use to make his case? Which of these arguments do you find most effective? Why?

Fears of Terrorist Attacks Are Exaggerated

Gavin de Becker

Gavin de Becker is an expert on security and terrorism who has worked closely with governments and private clients to predict and deal with possible attacks. In this excerpt from his book *Fear Less,* de Becker argues that fears of terrorism are exaggerated. He asserts that many predictions of terrorist attacks are based on little evidence and involve a poor understanding of the actual levels of risk. According to de Becker, it is extremely hard to carry out a large-scale terrorist attack, and the United States is generally well-prepared for the possibility.

Consider the following questions:

1. What is a worst-case scenario? What is its purpose? In de Becker's view, what is the value of a worst-case scenario?
2. According to de Becker, what factors make terrorist threats seem particularly real to present-day Americans?
3. How does de Becker say Americans should react to terrorism from Islamic radicals or other foreigners? How does he say Americans should react to terrorist attacks by their fellow Americans? What point is de Becker making in this part of his argument?

What's the bottom line?" people often ask me. "Will terrorists detonate a nuclear bomb? Spread smallpox? Release nerve gas? What's the worst-case scenario?"

Kirk. © 2004 by Kirk Anderson. Reproduced by permission.

You have probably known someone who experienced a trauma, then later seen that person reliving the tragedy. There is also such a thing as *pre-living* a tragedy. Exactly as we benefit from letting go of the past, millions of Americans will benefit from letting go of the worst-case future. Someone proposes a so-called worst-case scenario (as if there could be any objective view of what would constitute the worst case), and then the scenario gets discussed so much on television that it comes to seem like it's about to happen.

A worst-case scenario is a theoretical sequence of events intentionally devised to be as bad as possible, the word *scenario* coming from *scene,* as in a scene in a play or movie. Worst-case scenarios are creative exercises, not predictions of likely events. If we had examples of the realities to explore, we'd be doing that, but in most instances, we have only the imagination to chew on. Remember, these things enter the stream of discussion specifically because they are not likely, specifically because they are at the far end of possibility, and specifically because they have not ever happened.

These things start with someone saying, "Geez, what if terrorists got hold of an intercontinental ballistic missile?" Then TV news personalities interview experts in some loosely related field, a scary graphic is developed (say, a mushroom cloud emerging from the top of a local playground), then they hound a government official with the question "But isn't it possible that someone could get hold of an intercontinental ballistic missile?" and he says how unlikely that is, but acknowledges that it is possible (i.e., within the realm of physics and imagination)—and we're off and running.

The human mind pounces on this sort of thing because it can seem relevant to survival. We're hard-wired to entertain every thought of danger that's put in front of us, to turn it over, to look at it from every angle. The more enormous a lethal danger might be and the more people it might harm, the more fascinating it is. But for us to be fascinated by something, it has to be made accessible to our minds. For example, Earth coming out of its orbit and spinning off into a collision with Jupiter is too hard for us to get our minds around, but the idea of someone using a makeshift nuclear bomb has been made to appear plausible simply because of so much discussion.

Though TV news carries theoretical discussions of doom further than other media, magazines and newspapers do their part. Journalists are writers, and they love creative stories, so we get detailed accounts of precisely how terrible a terrible outcome could be. Editors love a dramatic hook, and you're the fish they're trying to catch with it. Print may seem to give credibility to worst-case scenarios, but the truth is that only you decide what credibility to invest in any given doomsday tale.

You've probably heard that anyone can easily get information about how to build a nuclear bomb by just logging

> ## The Threat of Terrorism Is Exaggerated
>
> There will always be terrorists and legitimate efforts to catch and kill them. But meanwhile, the bigger statistical threat comes from the driver next to you who is talking on the cell phone.
>
> Bart Kosko, "Terror Threat May Be Mostly a Big Bluff," *Los Angeles Times*, September 13, 2004.

In 2002 Homeland Security director Tom Ridge unveils the color-coded terrorism alert system, designed to help Americans assess the threat of terrorism at any given time.

on to the Internet. Have you tried "just logging on to the Internet" and getting those simple step-by-step instructions? Do you know how to build a nuclear bomb? Whenever I hear about how easy it is, I am reminded of an old routine from the brilliant humorist, author, and filmmaker Steve Martin: He would promise to tell his audience the secret of how one could earn a million dollars and yet pay absolutely *no* taxes. "First," he'd say as if this were the easy part, "earn a million dollars." To all those who make nuclear-bomb construction sound as simple as putting up Christmas lights, I'd say, "First, get some plutonium or highly enriched uranium."

Someday some person or group may indeed detonate a small nuclear device somewhere on earth. It will be awful. It will harm some people. It will be recovered from.

After we accept that it could happen, is it constructive to spend every day between now and then trying to experience the event in our minds?

The future is longer than the past, and because the future occurs on the foundation of the past, more will happen than has happened. This means that nearly everything we can imagine has some likelihood of happening sometime, particularly if you include far-off times. In a truly intelligent worst-case scenario, one would theorize that some young Americans bent on grand mischief are far more dangerous than foreign terrorists. They are here, they are brilliant, some are reckless, some are homicidal and suicidal; and we must assume that the extraordinary knowledge being accumulated in our society and made available to young people will be misused. Many teenagers are capable of mounting ferocious attacks and many have the motivation to do so—as we have learned from tragedies like [the 1999 school shootings in] Columbine [Colorado]. What a thirty-year-old would find discouragingly difficult to accomplish, an eighteen-year-old will keep trying. What a thirty-year-old might find too reckless or dangerous, an eighteen-year-old might find intriguing.

I make this point to bring some perspective during a time when Americans have focused almost entirely on Middle Eastern terrorists. When anthrax spores were sent through the mail after 9/11, we were fascinated to know if the crime was linked to the attack on the World Trade Center. This raises one of the most salient questions about risk: *Does motive matter?* It's understandable that people are more afraid if anthrax spores are sent by Middle Eastern terrorists, even though there are far more American-bred attention-seekers who might do this kind of thing. Excessive fascination with motive and with the origins of risk can cloud our ability to make an effective assessment of what is really likely and how to respond to events that actually occur. Whether sent by an American or a Middle Easterner, the best management of the anthrax cases remains the same.

There are people whose jobs require some degree of worst-case thinking. I am one of them. Whole teams of

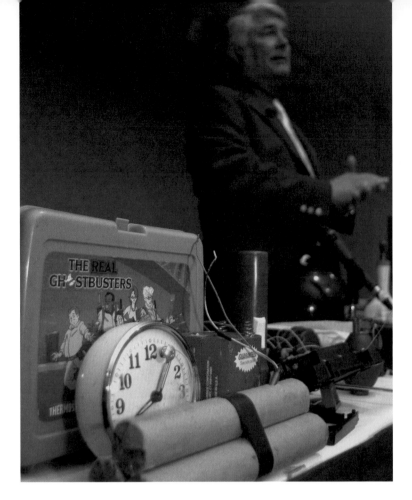

An investigator with the Arkansas State Bomb Squad speaks in 2005 on how emergency workers should respond in the event of a terrorist attack.

threat-assessment practitioners in my firm spend their time developing contingency plans and responses to cover a variety of unfavorable outcomes. For example, making arrangements for a controversial public figure to give a speech at a rally about an emotionally charged political issue calls for contingency plans about many kinds of things that could happen, but we put more effort into those possibilities that are most likely.

An assassin in the audience, at the vehicle-arrival area, or along the foot route from the car to the holding room; a sniper in the distance; a bomb that was placed a week before the event; someone trying to strike the public figure; even a pie attack—all these things and more are on our list during the days of planning leading up to such an appearance. I do not oppose contingency planning. I do oppose time wasting, however, and in my firm, in my life, and in your life, everything we give energy to takes energy away from something else. Accordingly, we are wisest to put our resources where they'll be most likely to return some benefit.

You already live your life according to that equation, deciding where to put your protective resources at home, for example. Though intruders could land a helicopter on your roof and come through the ceiling, you've decided that entry via the front door is more likely—and you've got a lock that requires a key. A criminal could photograph your credit cards with a telephoto lens and then painstakingly duplicate them, but you've determined that someone taking your purse is more likely—so you watch it carefully. If there's an emergency phone list in your home, the names and numbers reflect your family's assessment of likely hazards. Is the U.S. Department of Energy Nuclear Emergency Search Team on that list? Probably not, and you're not likely to need that phone number. You also have a list in your head of things you want to avoid or prevent. You base the list on experience, logic, new information, and intuition. The list has limits—*because it has to.*

Conversely, worst-case scenarios have no limits. Wherever the imagination can travel, your mind can take you there. But the trip is voluntary—even when TV news producers are urging you to go, you don't have to.

Analyze the essay:

1. In this essay de Becker draws a distinction between what *could* happen and what is *likely* to happen. How does drawing this distinction help him make his case? What possible objections to this argument might there be?

2. De Becker relates terrorism to everyday concerns such as the possibility of being the victim of credit card theft or burglary. What is his purpose in making this connection? Do you find his analogies convincing? Why or why not?

The U.S. Government Should Treat Terror Suspects Harshly

Heather MacDonald

In this essay columnist Heather MacDonald argues that getting information from suspected terrorists is critical to American safety. She asserts that concern for the rights of prisoners has made it difficult for interrogators to get this information. In MacDonald's opinion, prisoners should be subjected to threats of violence and similar "stress techniques" if they refuse to tell what they know, even if these techniques violate the terms of the Geneva Convention—an internationally approved guideline for the treatment of prisoners.

Consider the following questions:

1. According to MacDonald, why did so few terrorists captured in Afghanistan "break" upon being questioned?
2. In MacDonald's view, why does the U.S. government sharply limit acceptable interrogation techniques?
3. What does MacDonald mean by "stress techniques"?

Soon after the Afghanistan fighting began [in late 2001] Army interrogators realized that their part in the war on terror was not going according to script. Pentagon doctrine, honed in the Cold War, held that 95% of prisoners would break upon straightforward questioning. But virtually no al Qaeda and Taliban detainee was giving up information—not in response to direct questioning, and not in response to Army-approved psychological gambits for prisoners of war.

Some al Qaeda fighters had received resistance training, which taught that Americans were strictly limited in how they could question prisoners. Failure to cooperate, they had learned, carried no penalties and certainly no risk of torture—a sign, al Qaeda said, of American weakness. Even if a prisoner had not previously studied U.S. detention policies, he soon figured them out. "It became very clear very early on to the detainees that the Americans were just going to have them sit there," explains an Afghanistan interrogator. "They realized: 'The Americans will give us our Holy Book, they'll draw lines on the floor showing us where to pray, we'll get three meals a day with fresh fruit . . . we can wait them out.'" Traditional appeals to a prisoner's emotions, such as playing on his love of family or life, had little effect. "The jihadists would tell you, 'I've divorced this life, I don't care about my family,'" recalls an interrogator at Guantánamo Bay, Cuba.

Asay. © 2005 by Creators Syndicate, Inc. Reproduced by permission.

Frustrated interrogators across the globe concluded that their best hope for getting information was to re-create the "shock of capture"—that vulnerable mental state when a prisoner is most uncertain and most likely to respond to questioning. Many argued for a calibrated use of "stress techniques"—prolonged questioning that would cut into a detainee's sleep schedule, for example, or making a prisoner kneel or stand.

A crack interrogator from Afghanistan explains the psychological effect of stress: "Let's say a detainee comes into the interrogation booth and he's had resistance training. He knows that I'm completely handcuffed and that I can't do anything to him. If I throw a temper tantrum, lift him onto his knees, and walk out, you can feel his uncertainty level rise dramatically. He's been told: 'They won't physically touch you,' and now you have. The point is not to beat him up but to introduce the reality into his mind that he doesn't know where your limit is." Grabbing someone by the top of the collar has had a more profound effect on the outcome of questioning than any actual torture could have, this Army reservist maintains. "The guy knows: You just broke your own rules and that's scary."

Such treatment, though far short of torture, probably violates the Geneva Convention's norms for lawful prisoners of war, who must be protected from "any form of coercion." But terrorists fail every test for coverage under the Geneva Conventions: They seek to massacre civilians, they conceal their status as warriors, and they treat their own prisoners to such niceties as beheadings. President [George W.] Bush properly found that terrorists do not qualify as Geneva-protected prisoners of war.

In April 2003, the Pentagon finalized the rules for questioning unlawful combatants in Cuba, following a fierce six-month debate. The approved techniques were in many respects more restrictive than the Geneva Conventions themselves. Providing a detainee an incentive for cooperation—a McDonald's Filet-O-Fish sandwich or a Twinkie, say—was forbidden unless specifically cleared by the secretary of defense, because not every prisoner

A marine stationed in Guantánamo Bay, Cuba, displays restraining devices used when transporting detainees.

An interrogator monitors soldiers as they participate in mock interrogation sessions. Such exercises are designed to teach soldiers appropriate interrogation techniques.

would receive the goodie. Other long-standing army psychological techniques, such as attacking a detainee's pride or the classic good cop/bad cop routine, also required a specific finding of military necessity and notice to Donald Rumsfeld.

The only nonconventional "stress" techniques on the final Guantánamo list are such innocuous interventions as adjusting the temperature or introducing an unpleasant smell into the interrogation room (but only if the interrogator is present at all times), reversing a detainee's sleep cycles from night to day, and convincing a detainee that his interrogator is not from the U.S. And those mild techniques could only be used with extensive bureaucratic oversight and medical monitoring to ensure "humane," "safe," and "lawful" application. . . .

In the wake of the Abu Ghraib disaster [in which American prison guards in Iraq were found to have tortured prisoners] and the ensuing media storm, the Pentagon has shut down every stress technique but one—isolation—and that can be used only after extensive review. An interrogator who so much as requests permission to question a detainee into the night could be putting his career in jeopardy. Interrogation plans have to be triple-checked all the way up through the Pentagon by bureaucrats who have never conducted an interrogation in their lives.

To succeed in the war on terror, interrogators must be allowed to use carefully controlled stress techniques against unlawful combatants. Stress works, say interrogators. The techniques that the military has used to date come nowhere near torture; the advocates can only be posturing in calling them such. These self-professed guardians of humanitarianism need to come back to earth. Our terrorist enemies have declared themselves enemies of the civilized order. In fighting them, we must hold ourselves to our own high moral standards—without succumbing to the utopian illusion that we can prevail while immaculately observing every precept of the Sermon on the Mount.

Analyze the essay:

1. MacDonald argues that the Geneva Convention should not apply to terror suspects. How does she support her argument? Do you find her evidence convincing? Why or why not?
2. What point is MacDonald making in her last sentence? How does she characterize those who disagree with her?

The U.S. Government Should Treat Terror Suspects Humanely

Jeff Jacoby

Boston Globe columnist Jeff Jacoby argues in this essay that U.S. interrogators should never use torture techniques against suspected terrorists. While acknowledging the desire for revenge and the need for information about terrorist activities, Jacoby insists that international laws forbid the use of force against terror suspects. Moreover, he says, violence should never be met with violence. Jacoby's column was written in March 2005, soon after widespread allegations of prisoner abuse appeared in the American media.

Consider the following questions:

1. What is the Convention Against Torture? In Jacoby's opinion, why does it apply to the United States and its treatment of terror suspects?
2. According to Jacoby, what is the "ticking-bomb" scenario? What does it have to do with the question of whether terror suspects should be subjected to torture?
3. On what grounds does Jacoby ultimately reject the use of torture against terror suspects?

The Convention Against Torture and Other Cruel, Inhuman, or Degrading Treatment or Punishment, which the United States ratified in 1994, prohibits the torture of any person for any reason by any government

at any time. It states explicitly that torture is never justified—"no exceptional circumstances whatsoever . . .
may be invoked as a justification for torture." Unlike the
Geneva Convention, which protects legitimate prisoners
of war, the Convention Against Torture applies to every-
one—even terrorists and enemy combatants. And it may
not be evaded—this is spelled out in Article 3—by "out-
sourcing" a prisoner to a country where he is apt to be
tortured during interrogation.

In short, the international ban on torture—a ban incor-
porated into US law—is absolute. And before Sept. 11,
2001, few Americans would have argued that it should
be anything else.

But in post-9/11 America, the unthinkable is not only
being thought, but openly considered. And not only by
hawks on the right, but even by critics in the center and
on the left.

Source: Parker. © 2004 by Cagle Cartoons, Inc. Reproduced by permission.

"In this autumn of anger," Jonathan Alter commented in *Newsweek* not long after the terrorist attacks, "a liberal can find his thoughts turning to—torture." Maybe cattle prods and rubber hoses should remain off-limits, he wrote, but "some torture clearly works," and Americans had to "keep an open mind" about using unconventional measures—including "transferring some suspects to our less squeamish allies."

In March 2003, a few days after arch-terrorist Khalid Sheikh Mohammed was captured in Pakistan, [columnist] Stuart Taylor Jr. surmised that Mohammed was probably being made to feel some pain. "And if that's the best chance of making him talk, it's OK by me," he wrote in his *National Journal* column. In principle, interrogators should not cross the line into outright torture. But, Taylor continued, "my answer might be different in extreme circumstances."

Suspects Must Never Be Tortured

The prohibition of torture and cruel, inhumane, or degrading treatment or punishment is absolute and unconditional, in peace or in war. This dehumanizing practice is always wrong.

Kenneth Roth, "Time to Stop 'Stress and Duress,'" *Washington Post*, May 13, 2004, p. A29.

By "extreme circumstances" he meant what is often called the "ticking-bomb" scenario: A deadly terror attack is looming, and you can prevent it only by getting the information your prisoner refuses to divulge. Torture might force him to talk, thereby saving thousands of innocent lives. Should he be tortured?

Many Americans would say yes without hesitating. Some would argue that torturing a terrorist is not nearly as wrong as refusing to do so and thereby allowing another 9/11 to occur. Others would insist that monsters of Mohammed's ilk deserve no decency.

As an indignant reader (one of many) wrote to me after last week's column on the cruel abuse of some US detainees, "The terrorists . . . would cut your heart out and stuff it into the throat they would proudly slash

In August 2004 Michael Rattner, president of the Center for Constitutional Rights, holds a report that alleges Guantánamo Bay prisoners have been physically abused by U.S. soldiers.

open." So why not torture detainees, if it will produce the information we need?

Here's why:

First, because torture, as noted, is unambiguously illegal—illegal under a covenant the United States ratified, illegal under federal and military law, and illegal under protocols of civilization dating back to the Magna Carta [a British legal document of 1215].

Second, because torture is notoriously unreliable. Many people will say anything to make the pain stop, while some will refuse to yield no matter what is done to them. Yes, sometimes torture produces vital information. But it can also produce false leads and desperate fictions. In

the ticking-bomb case, bad information is every bit as deadly as no information.

Third, because torture is never limited to just the guilty. The case for razors and electric shock rests on the premise that the prisoner is a knowledgeable terrorist like KSM [Khalid Sheikh Muhammad] or Abu Musab al-Zarqawi [a Jordanian radical possibly linked to al Qaeda]. But most of the detainees in US military prisons are nothing of the kind. Commanders in Guántanamo [an American military base used for prisoner detention] acknowledge that hundreds of their prisoners pose no danger and have no useful information. How much of the hideous abuse reported to date involved men who were guilty only of being in the wrong place at the wrong time?

And fourth, because torture is a dangerously slippery slope. Electric shocks and beatings are justified, you may say, if they can prevent another 9/11. But what if the shocks and beating don't produce the needed information? Is it OK to break a finger? To cut off a hand? In order to save 3,000 lives, can a terrorist's eyes be gouged out? How about gouging out his son's eyes? Or raping his daughter in his presence? If that's what it will take to make him talk, to defuse the ticking bomb, isn't it worth it?

No. Torture is never worth it. Some things we don't do, not because they never work, not because they aren't "deserved," but because our very right to call ourselves decent human beings depends in part on our not doing them. Torture is in that category. Let us wage and win this war against the barbarians without becoming barbaric in the process.

Analyze the essay:

1. Jacoby compares American attitudes toward torture both before and after September 11, 2001. What is his purpose in making this comparison?
2. To what extent does Jacoby base his argument on ethics and moral reasoning? Do you find his use of moral reasoning persuasive? Why or why not?

Section Two:
Model Essays
and Writing
Exercises

Writing the Persuasive Five-Paragraph Essay

The viewpoints and articles that appear in the previous section all give the opinions of the writers. The authors attempt to convince, or persuade, their readers to accept their arguments. These types of essays are known as persuasive essays; they are written in support of a particular idea. In this section you will work on writing a persuasive essay of your own.

Examples of persuasive writing are easy to find. Advertising is one common example. Through commercials and print ads, companies try to convince the public to buy certain sports drinks, wear particular brands of sneakers, and drive specific models of cars. Much everyday writing is persuasive, too. Letters to the editor, posts from sports fans on team Web sites, even handwritten notes urging a friend to listen to a new CD—all are examples of persuasive writing.

Persuasive writing relies on making an argument, also known as a thesis statement. It is in the author's interest to make this argument as clearly and carefully as possible. As a result, writers of persuasive essays usually state their thesis early in the piece. Most often, the thesis appears in the opening paragraph. The first sentence of Viewpoint 5, for example, neatly sums up Stephen Flynn's position on American preparedness. When an author of a persuasive essay chooses to begin with an anecdote or with background introductory material, as Cal Thomas does in Viewpoint 3, the thesis is still easy to find and typically appears somewhere in the first few paragraphs of the article.

Supporting Evidence

The thesis statement is an essential part of a persuasive essay, but it is not the only part. A persuasive essay must not only present an argument, but it also must give reasons why a reader should accept the argument. The heart of a persuasive essay, then, presents the evidence that backs up the thesis statement.

Evidence for a thesis can come from several different sources. Many writers present factual information that supports their case. In Viewpoint 5, for instance, Flynn describes how easy and cheap it can be for terrorists to acquire weapons in some parts of the world. By making it clear that terrorists have no trouble arming themselves, this piece of information strengthens Flynn's claim that terrorism is a serious threat.

Facts can often include quotes from experts and others with specialized information, too. In Viewpoint 2, for instance, Bob Herbert cites the words of military officials responsible for monitoring the progress of the war in Iraq. Sometimes personal information and anecdotes are used as well. Nicholas D. Kristof in Viewpoint 4 relies on his own conversations with a white supremacist to express his concerns about Matt Hale and his followers. Statistics, too, can be important in persuasive writing. In Viewpoint 3, for example, Cal Thomas points out that a sizable percentage of people responsible for one terror attack had links to al Qaeda and similar organizations.

Facts, statistics, and quotations from experts are all important in persuasive writing—but they should be used *only* to back up a thesis and illustrate an argument. In Viewpoint 4, for instance, Kristof mentions the case of William Krar, a militia member found to have a large supply of weapons and poisons. Kristof describes the entire case in one brief sentence. The details of Krar's case are not important to Kristof's thesis. Instead, Kristof refers to the case simply to show that members of domestic groups may be inclined toward violence.

Opposing Perspectives

While a good persuasive essay focuses mainly on the author's opinion, most persuasive essays mention alternate views as well.

It may seem odd to present opposing viewpoints in a piece of persuasive writing, but, in fact, there are good reasons to do so. For one, it is wise for a writer to anticipate and acknowledge the possible objections to his or her thesis, especially when many people hold this opposing belief. Many Americans, for instance, would say that torture is a legitimate tactic to use against terror suspects. If Jeff Jacoby had not acknowledged this reality in his viewpoint, some readers might have dismissed Jacoby's position altogether. It would have seemed as if Jacoby was presenting only the facts that supported his case and ignoring arguments to the contrary. By mentioning the opposing perspective, Jacoby made it clear that he had thought about the question from all sides.

Moreover, writers can often strengthen their arguments by presenting and then criticizing alternative viewpoints. In Viewpoint 3, for instance, Thomas describes Omar Bakri Mohammed's viewpoint on terrorism—and then explains exactly why he believes Mohammed's view to be misguided. By attacking Mohammed's perspective, Thomas not only argues that Mohammed is wrong, but he also builds his own case that radical Islam is the enemy.

Persuasive essays can be effective without mentioning alternative viewpoints, but they are generally more effective when they take note of other perspectives as well. Writers who take the time to acknowledge and respond to other viewpoints benefit considerably from the effort. The reader not only knows that the author has considered another point of view, but he or she also sees how the author has challenged and answered this opposing position. The result is usually a stronger and more convincing article.

The Five-Paragraph Essay

In the following section you will read model essays on the subject of terrorism, and you will practice writing essays of your own. This section of the book will focus on a particular type of essay known as the five-paragraph essay. As the name implies, the five-paragraph essay consists of five paragraphs, each roughly the same length. The first paragraph serves as an introduction. Like many of the viewpoints in the first section of this book, this paragraph presents the topic of the essay and explains why it is important. It also gives the thesis statement. In any five-paragraph essay, the thesis statement should be clear and easy to spot. Because persuasive essays are all about making and supporting arguments, a strong thesis statement is especially important in this kind of writing.

The introduction of a five-paragraph essay is followed by three supporting paragraphs. Together, these paragraphs make up the body of the essay. Each paragraph provides facts, figures, quotes from experts, or other evidence to back up the writer's thesis statement. Usually, each paragraph explores a separate argument, sometimes known as a subtopic. The supporting paragraphs are the heart of the essay; they determine whether the essay will be effective or not. Writers therefore need to be sure to find the best arguments in favor of their thesis, and they need to support their ideas with the best available evidence as well.

The final paragraph of a five-paragraph essay is the conclusion, sometimes known as the summary paragraph. The conclusion restates the thesis and summarizes the main arguments presented in the essay. On occasion, the conclusion may also go beyond the arguments in the essay and explore the larger context of the thesis. For instance, the conclusion may predict what will happen if changes in a government policy are not made or offer the reader a new way of thinking about the controversy.

As you read these model essays, pay careful attention to how they are structured. Look for thesis statements and topic sentences. Identify the thrust of each subtopic, and explore the types of supporting evidence used for each. Note the transitions between the paragraphs. Sometimes, arguments build on one another; other times, arguments are considered separately. Ask yourself how the introduction to each essay captures and holds the attention of the reader and how the conclusion serves to wrap up the argument and restate the thesis. Each essay includes sidebars that will help you identify these and other important features of the five-paragraph essay form.

Reaching Out to Muslim Nations Can Prevent Terrorism

Editor's Notes The following five-paragraph essay attempts to persuade the reader that reaching out to Muslim nations is a good way to prevent terrorism. The introduction establishes that the United States is a target of terrorism because it is unpopular in many parts of the Muslim world. The supporting paragraphs each offer one piece of evidence for why reaching out to Muslim nations would help prevent terrorism.

As you read this essay, take note of its components and how it is organized. In addition, consider the following questions:

1. How does the introduction engage the reader's attention?
2. What kinds of supporting evidence are used to back up the essay's arguments?
3. What purpose do the essay's quotes serve?
4. How does the author transition from one idea to another?

Not all terrorists are radical Muslims, of course, but there is no denying that Islamic militants are responsible for much of the terrorist activity in the world today. That is especially true of terrorist activity aimed against the United States. In many predominantly Muslim nations, large segments of the population hate the United States and all that it stands for. Under such conditions, it is no surprise that anti-American hostility has sometimes led to actual terrorist attacks. But it does not have to be this way. By reaching out to Muslims and Muslim nations worldwide, the United States could change the way the United States is perceived among its bitterest enemies. In this way, over time, the United States could dramatically reduce the threat of terrorism.

What is the purpose of the first sentence of the essay? How does it signal what is to come?

What is the thesis statement? How do you know?

One important reality of the Muslim world is that many of its people are in great need. Countries such as Mali, Somalia, and Bangladesh are poor and in turmoil. Hundreds of thousands of people in these nations lack even basic education and health care. For some, even finding enough to eat is an almost impossible challenge. The United States can use its resources to provide food, medicines, and money to build and equip schools. American diplomats can help national leaders create and carry out long-range plans; American agricultural specialists can help replace inefficient farming techniques; American investors can help local citizens establish small businesses. These efforts will cost money, to be sure, but the investment will pay off handsomely. By creating more stable governments and healthier economies, American outreach will gradually eliminate the desperate conditions that breed terrorism and terrorists. American assistance can reduce the anger and pain felt by millions around the globe, thereby offering the hope of a brighter future and steering people away from the use of violence.

Reaching out will help reduce the threat of terror in another way as well. Terrorists aim their attacks at countries they hate and despise. At present, the United States is viewed with suspicion, even with hatred, by many inhabitants of the world's poorest nations, particularly those that are predominantly Muslim. The people of these countries are aware of the enormous power and wealth of the United States, and they wonder why Americans devote so little of their resources to foreign assistance. Indeed, less than 1 percent of the U.S. budget goes to foreign aid. The result is that people in the Middle East and elsewhere often see America as a country that cares little for the world around it. By increasing outreach efforts and maintaining a compassionate presence in the poorest nations of the world, the United States can change that image to one of supporter and friend. If the people most likely to become terrorists grow up seeing the pos-

Citing problems with health care, education, and food supplies makes the problems less general and more immediate.

What specific actions does the essay suggest the United States carry out? How does this list help the essay make its point?

What is the purpose of the last sentence of this paragraph?

What words signal the transition to a new idea?

What is the topic sentence for the second supporting paragraph? Where does it appear?

itive good the United States can help create, the threat of terrorist attacks will certainly be reduced.

Finally, the consequences of not reaching out are potentially disastrous. Countries such as Somalia require urgent assistance. If the United States fails to help, nations and private interests that are hostile to America may very well do so instead. By ignoring the needs of the people of Afghanistan and Sudan, for example, the United States opened the door for al Qaeda forces to step in. And history is in danger of repeating itself. U.S. senator Russ Feingold writes of a crowd that lined the streets of Mali's largest city to cheer the arrival of the president of Iran, a country that has often been accused of giving aid to terrorists. If radical Islam offers these nations economic and political hope, then Islamic militants will be the winners. They, not Americans, will gain the trust and gratefulness of ordinary Muslims, and their harsh and angry rhetoric against the United States and its allies will be heard—and accepted—even more widely than it is today. To allow forces such as these to gain influence in the world's poorest countries is unthinkable; it can only hurt American efforts to forestall terrorist attacks.

The advantages of extending aid to the Muslim world, then, are clear. Not only is it the right thing to do, in humanitarian terms, it is also appropriate where the security of the United States is concerned. By reaching out to Muslim countries, the United States can ease conditions that create and encourage terrorism. It can win over peoples and governments who might otherwise be hostile toward America. And it can reduce the impact of forces that already hold a deep-rooted hatred of the United States. Indeed, reaching out to Muslim nations is one of the easiest, best, and most sensible approaches the United States can use to reduce the threat of terrorism.

What word tells the reader that this paragraph will provide the third and last supporting argument?

What facts are used to justify the argument in this paragraph?

This section looks ahead to what might happen in the future—a common feature of persuasive writing. What is its purpose?

How does the conclusion wrap up the arguments expressed earlier? Which sentence addresses each subtopic?

Choose a Topic and Create an Outline for a Persuasive Essay

The four exercises that follow will take you through the steps necessary to create your own persuasive essay. The first step in writing any essay is to choose the topic. For this group of exercises, you will need to choose a topic that is related in some way to terrorism or to the war on terror. Remember that you will be writing a persuasive essay, so it is important that you take a position on the topic you choose.

One possible topic would be to create a plan for winning the war on terror. For this essay, you would choose three important actions you believe the United States should take to defeat terrorists and protect the country from terrorist attacks. In this example, you would treat the three proposed actions as subtopics and devote a paragraph to each. A different possibility would be to focus on one particular action, such as improving airport security or making it harder to get driver's licenses. In this case, your essay would either support or disagree with the action. Alternatively, you could choose one of the opposing viewpoint arguments listed below:

- The war on terror is/is not being waged effectively
- Questioning the war on terror is a basic right/is unpatriotic
- Terrorism can be stopped/can never be stopped

Read through the viewpoints in Section 1 again to help you make your decision, and study the book's appendixes as well. Both sections will give you ideas for possible topics and the kinds of evidence you will need to support your perspective.

Once you have chosen your topic, the next step is to create an outline. Outlines give the thesis statement and list the major arguments of the essay in the order they will appear; you can also use an outline to summarize your supporting evidence. This part of the process focuses entirely on ideas and evidence, not on quality of writing; indeed, outlines are usually done in bullet form, so complete sentences are unnecessary. Nor are transitions and details of the arguments important at this stage. The purpose of an outline is simply to help organize your work and see how your ideas connect to one another. After making sure that your outline is complete and flows appropriately from one topic to the next, you can use the outline as a framework to help you write the essay.

Use the viewpoints in Section 1 and the appendix, your own ideas, and the bibliographies provided at the back of this book to create an outline that will provide the framework for a full-scale essay on your chosen topic. Remember that your essay is a persuasive essay; it must be designed to convince the reader that your argument is right. Use the form below.

Paragraph 1: Thesis Statement: _____
_____
_____
_____

Paragraph 2: First Argument: _____
_____
_____
_____

    Evidence: _____
    _____
    _____
    _____

Paragraph 3: Second Argument: _____
_____
_____
_____

Evidence: _____
_____
_____
_____
_____
_____

Paragraph 4: Third Argument: _____
_____
_____

Evidence: _____
_____
_____
_____
_____
_____

Paragraph 5: Conclusion: _____
_____
_____

Reaching Out to Muslim Nations Will Not Prevent Terrorism

Editor's Notes The second five-paragraph essay takes an opposing view to the first model essay: It argues that reaching out to Muslim nations will not prevent terrorism. To do this, the author challenges the evidence put forth in the first essay. The essay's conclusion does not merely repeat the ideas presented in the essay but ties the information together and makes an observation about the realities of the terrorist problem.

The notes in the sidebars provide questions that will help you analyze how this essay is organized and how it is written.

It is tempting to believe that simply increasing the amount of aid and attention given to Muslim countries can help reduce the threat of terrorism. Certainly this hope is well intentioned—and it would be wonderful if it were the case. Unfortunately, however, the reasoning behind this argument is flawed. In fact, further reaching out to Muslim nations will do very little to reduce the threat of terrorism. In the past, American foreign aid has not succeeded in stopping anti-American terrorist groups from carrying out attacks. Nor is poverty linked as closely to terrorism as some observers wish to believe. Indeed, the root causes of radical Islamic terrorism lie not in poverty but in a fanatical religious hatred of America—an irrational hatred that, sadly, cannot be destroyed simply through gifts and kindness. Reaching out to Muslim nations, then, will do little or nothing to end the threat of terrorism.

Although some accuse the United States of not providing enough assistance and support to poorer nations around the globe, the truth is that the United States is a leader in providing foreign aid. Predominantly Muslim

> How does the first sentence introduce the topic of the essay? What technique is being used here, and why?

> Which sentences introduce possible subtopics?

> What is the function of the last sentence of the paragraph?

> What idea is discredited in the first sentence of this paragraph?

nations such as Jordan and Pakistan receive hundreds of millions of dollars from the United States annually; even Saudi Arabia, a relatively wealthy country due to vast oil reserves, benefits from American assistance programs. Yet the enormous quantities of money spent on aid to these nations have not dissuaded terrorists from lashing out at the United States. It was a Pakistani terrorist, Ramzi Yousef, who planned the detonation of a car bomb beneath the World Trade Center in 1993; and most of the September 11 hijackers were Saudi Arabian citizens. Nor has aid kept Muslim religious and government leaders from offering encouragement and support to terrorists. There is no reason to expect that adding to American aid programs will change the minds of the people who hate the United States.

Those who endorse the idea that aid will help often attribute terrorism to the poverty of the Muslim world. It is certainly true that many predominantly Islamic nations are desperately poor. Countries such as Niger and Somalia have high infant mortality rates, low life expectancies, and severely limited opportunities for education and jobs. But the relationship between poverty and terrorism is overstated. Al Qaeda leader Osama bin Laden, after all, was very far from a child of the lower class—on the contrary, he was a multimillionaire. Muhammad Atta, the man who masterminded the September 11 terrorist attack, grew up in comfort as the son of an Egyptian lawyer. And Saudi Arabia, the home of most of the terrorists who carried out the hijackings, is one of the wealthiest nations in the Middle East. As these examples indicate, it is simply inaccurate to say that terrorism is caused by poverty. Consequently, throwing money at impoverished countries will not eliminate the problem of terrorism.

Indeed, the United States can do very little to ease the problem of Islamic terrorists. The fact is that Muslim terrorism is created not by economic conditions but by political and religious fanaticism. Many radical Muslims see the secular West, with its consumer culture and its emphasis on women's rights, as decadent and irreligious—and they believe themselves to be engaged in a jihad, or holy war, against the non-Muslim governments of countries like America. While these radicals do not make up the majority of Muslims, they hold an influence in the Islamic world that goes far beyond their numbers. "Our terrorist sons," writes Arab Muslim Abdulrahman al-Rashed, quoted by political columnist Cal Thomas, "are an end-product of our corrupted culture." It is the responsibility of moderate Muslims like al-Rashed to rein in these terrorists and to declare unequivocally that terrorism is not an acceptable part of Islam. Until they do so, the United States is powerless to stop the spread of terrorism throughout the Muslim world.

There is, of course, nothing wrong with extending assistance to poor Muslim countries such as Chad and Bangladesh. But aid given on humanitarian grounds must be distinguished from aid intended to win friends and reduce the threat of terrorist attack. In truth, even if the United States had the will and the ability to solve all of the pressing financial and governmental problems faced by these nations, it would not be enough. "Even the wisest, kindest, and gentlest American leadership," writes government official Stephen Flynn, "will not appease groups like the remnants of the Taliban, whose beliefs are the antithesis of our own." In fact, hostility toward America in these nations has nothing to do with the realities of U.S. policy. If America did not cause terrorism, then America is powerless to solve the problem. That, instead, must be the responsibility of the Muslim world.

Why do you think the subtopics are presented in this order? How do they build on one another?

A quote is used here to provide the opinion of an expert, in this case a Muslim whose ideas match those of the writer of the essay.

According to the essay, how can terrorism be stopped, if not through American aid?

The conclusion offers a new idea not fully developed in the body of the essay. What is that idea? Why is it important?

Write an Introduction

In this exercise you will use the outline you created in the previous exercise and write an introduction to an essay. The introduction should be based on the thesis statement and the supporting arguments that you chose for your outline.

First, reread the opening sections of all eight viewpoints in Section 1. (Remember, in these viewpoints the introductory section sometimes consists of more than one paragraph.) Read over the introductions for the first two model essays as well. Which introductions do you find most effective? Why? Identify which introductions are written especially clearly, which are the most successful in grabbing the reader's attention, and which do the best job of explaining why the topic is important. Then consider how you can use these qualities in your own essay.

As you reread the introductions to these viewpoints and model essays, you may notice several particularly effective techniques. These may include the following:

- Facts and statistics, especially ones that engage the reader emotionally, which relate in some way to the topic of the essay and the thesis statement. (See, for example, Jeff Jacoby's opening sentence in Viewpoint 8.)
- Stories and anecdotes that illustrate important points connected to the topic. (Nicholas D. Kristof's interview with Matt Hale does this effectively in Viewpoint 4.)
- Using the thesis statement as the first sentence of the introduction, particularly when it is expressed in strong and provocative language. (Stephen Flynn opens Viewpoint 5 in exactly this way.)

- Introducing the topic by asking questions that serve to draw the reader in and which the reader expects will be answered later in the essay. (Gavin de Becker uses this method in Viewpoint 6.)
- Presenting an opposing argument that you will quickly knock down. (Model Essay 2 provides a good example of this technique.)

Note that it is not necessary to use the thesis statement as the opening sentence of an essay. You probably found that most introductions did not use this technique. In writing a persuasive essay, it is generally better to begin the essay by drawing the reader in and appealing to his or her emotions. However, the thesis statement does need to appear in the introduction, and keep in mind that the introduction must be contained within the first paragraph of a five-paragraph essay.

Now, write an introduction for the essay you outlined in Exercise 1. Be aware of which three subtopics, or arguments, you intend to use in the essay; this will help you shape your introduction. Include at least four sentences in your paragraph, more if necessary. Make sure that each sentence has a good reason for being a part of the introduction, and that the sentences flow smoothly from one idea to the next. Read your finished work aloud to be sure your paragraph makes sense. Then take a moment to double-check punctuation, capitalization, and spelling.

Essay Three

Strict Antiterrorism Measures Are Necessary to Make America Safer

Editor's Notes This essay is longer than five paragraphs. Sometimes five paragraphs are simply not enough to adequately develop an idea. Extending the length of an essay can allow the reader to explore a topic in more depth or present multiple pieces of evidence that together provide a more complete picture of a topic. Longer essays can also help readers discover the complexity of a subject. Notice, though, that the structure of the longer essay is actually not very different from the form of the five-paragraph essays that appeared earlier in this section. As you read the model essay, pay close attention to the similarities and differences in the styles and formats of the essays of different lengths.

While you read, consider the questions posed in the margins. Continue to identify thesis statements, supporting details, transitions, and quotations. Examine the introductory and concluding paragraphs to understand how they give shape to the essay. Finally, evaluate the essay's general structure and assess its overall effectiveness.

What is the purpose of the opening sentence?

The United States has a long and proud history as an open society in which government forces do not keep a close eye on the movements and activities of its people. There is much to be said for this approach. But in a modern world, where terrorism has become the major threat to the safety and security of Americans, it is unconscionable to continue these hands-off policies. To protect the people of the United States from attack, government officials must adopt stronger and stricter antiterrorism measures. Americans may be inconvenienced by some of these measures; a few people may even argue that these policies are a violation of civil liberties. In the face of mounting terrorist threats, however, concerns about convenience and rights

Which sentence is the thesis statement? Note that it does not appear at the beginning of the introduction.

80

must not interfere with the nation's first priority: protecting its citizens from terrorist attacks.

Strict antiterrorism measures may take a number of different forms. Most are simple enough to implement; all are reasonable and logical. To prevent a repeat of the September 11, 2001, hijacking disaster, for example, airline passengers must be subjected to rigorous weapons searches before they are allowed to board. Similarly, government officials must have quick access to library and banking records of people suspected of being terrorists or supporting terrorist groups. Law enforcement officers need the power to inspect the homes or offices of potential terrorists without informing the suspects that they are under investigation. And in some cases, especially when the threat of terrorist attack may be imminent, it could even prove necessary to arrest suspected terrorists and hold them for a time without formally charging them or giving them access to a lawyer. These and other counterterrorism measures help ensure the public safety. To fail to implement them would be to allow terrorists easy opportunities to destroy American society.

There is ample evidence that our relaxed attitude toward security has created opportunities for terrorist activity in the past. The events leading up to the September 11 hijackings are an excellent case in point. Stricter, more thorough airport screenings, for instance, would have revealed the weapons the terrorists were carrying. Moreover, closer monitoring of the hijackers might have revealed distressing information about their activities—for example, that they were in communication with known terrorists, that some were taking flying lessons, even that they were behaving suspiciously while using computers at public libraries. But the lax measures in place at the time made it impossible to prevent the attacks that followed. And according to government official Stephen Flynn, the situation is no better today. "The measures we have been cobbling together," Flynn writes, "are hardly fit to deter amateur thieves, vandals, and [computer] hackers, never mind determined terrorists."

> This paragraph does not express an argument. Instead, it offers examples of antiterrorism measures. Its purpose is to give a context to the arguments that follow.

> The examples given are drawn from a broad range of possible antiterrorism measures. How are they arranged and organized in this paragraph?

> What is the topic sentence of this paragraph? How do you know the paragraph presents an argument?

> What specific examples are given to support this argument? What measures are suggested by each?

> The end of the paragraph marks a transition from a discussion of the past to a discussion of today.

Some people complain that stricter antiterrorism laws could infringe upon civil liberties. In truth, these concerns are wildly exaggerated. Most proposed measures have no impact whatever on the basic rights of Americans. One reason is that government officials have long used the power to search the homes and to probe the financial records of certain suspects, as in cases of drug trafficking and organized crime; extending these powers to combat terrorism is nothing new. As former attorney general Edwin Meese III puts it, "Most of the steps taken after September 11 to combat terrorism follow those previously authorized to fight serious criminal activity." Moreover, these measures may only be used when law enforcement officials have good reason to suspect a person of being active in a terrorist group. People who follow the law have nothing to fear from such measures.

But even if strict antiterrorism measures were a potential violation of ordinary Americans' civil rights, it would still be necessary to implement them. Terrorism represents the single greatest challenge to America today. If Americans relax their guard against the dangers of terror, the next attack could make the September 11, 2001, disaster seem tiny in comparison. Imagine groups of terrorists entering the United States and planning a series of simultaneous attacks on bridges, tunnels, city centers, and government buildings across America. Imagine government officials being barred from taking the necessary steps to stop these actions, all because a few Americans worry that these measures might interfere with someone's civil liberties. And now, imagine the carnage and the destruction as bombs explode throughout this country. Forced to choose between protecting civil rights and ensuring security and survival for millions of Americans, government officials must choose the latter.

It would be wonderful if America could go back to a more innocent time, a time when measures such as these were unnecessary. It is certainly an inconvenience for Americans to have to submit to close inspections when boarding an airplane or to know that their library records can be made available to law enforcement officials. But the demands of these and other antiterrorism measures place only a small burden on law-abiding Americans, especially when compared to the benefits of such policies. If by instituting strict antiterrorism measures the United States can prevent just one deadly attack, then any inconvenience will have been well worth the effort.

How is the essay's thesis restated in the conclusion? What differences and similarities are there between the introduction and the closing paragraph?

Exercise Three

Write Supporting Paragraphs

In this exercise you will write three supporting paragraphs for the essay you outlined in Exercise 1 and began writing in Exercise 2.

First, go back to your original outline. Look again at the list of arguments you created when you made the outline. While you were writing the introduction, you may have thought of new ideas or new arguments. That is fine; an outline is not a completed document and should be changed whenever you have new and better ideas. Make alterations to the outline, if necessary; then look over your new outline to be certain that your new plan makes sense. Do the same with the evidence you listed in the outline. Is there new evidence you might consider using? Are there counterarguments that you might wish to include?

Once you are satisfied with all the parts of your outline, you can begin to write. Start with your first argument, which will be given in the paragraph right after the introduction. If your outline is a good one, the writing of this paragraph should be fairly easy. Begin by rewriting the argument so that it is no longer in bullet form but is expressed, instead, as a complete sentence. Then rewrite your evidence in complete sentences, too. Add transitional words and phrases (*in addition, moreover, however,* and *although* are helpful) and sentences as necessary to make the paragraph a meaningful whole. Reread the first three model essays for further ideas about how to put this argument together. It is often wise to close the paragraph with a summarizing sentence, such as the one found in the middle paragraph of Model Essay 2.

Repeat the process for the second and third arguments. Remember, a good outline already contains most of the information you will need to write a good paragraph. Again, pay close attention to how your ideas are worded and how they are connected. As you write, you may discover that you need further evidence, or perhaps you will need a higher level of detail for some of the arguments you present. You may also discover that you have more detail than you actually need. Be sure that every sentence has a purpose, and that each idea relates directly to your argument and the topic sentence of your paragraph.

Once you have written all three paragraphs, read them over again, aloud if possible. Add transitional words and phrases to provide a natural flow from one argument to the next. Ideally, all three paragraphs should be of similar lengths, but it is more important that they all be the right length to make your argument clear and convincing. Be sure your writing is as vivid as possible, too; a reader who is bored by your essay is not likely to find the arguments persuasive! As before, review the viewpoints and the model essays for ideas to help you do this.

Strict Antiterrorism Measures Violate Civil Liberties

Editor's Notes Like the other essays you have read, the final model essay establishes its main idea up front, uses supporting paragraphs that provide evidence for the thesis, and concludes with a paragraph that wraps up the information that has been presented. As you read, pay attention to the ways in which the author tries to persuade you of his point of view. What devices work particularly well in making his case? What pieces of evidence are especially compelling, and why?

Understanding effective methods of persuasion will help you write your own persuasive essay in Exercise 4. It is important to note that you do not necessarily have to approach the construction of your essay in the order that has been presented here. Some writers prefer to write their introduction first and then tackle the three subtopics that make up the body of the essay. Others find it more helpful to write their subtopics before returning to flesh out the opening paragraph. There is no one recipe for writing a five-paragraph essay; writers must decide for themselves what methods work best.

These are uneasy times. The despicable terrorist attacks of September 11, 2001, have brought the reality of terrorism home to all Americans. Threats of further violence are received daily by government officials and law enforcement officers across the country. Ordinary citizens find themselves worrying about unattended backpacks, whispered cell phone conversations, strangers speaking in an unfamiliar language. Fears of terrorism are everywhere; and they are justified. Clearly, America has powerful, angry enemies who are eager to destroy it.

Following September 11 many Americans—including a number of influential political figures—have advocated strict measures to combat the threat of terrorism. They

The introduction to this essay spans the first three paragraphs. What is the purpose of each of the three?

What examples are given here? What words are used to play on the reader's emotions?

The word *however* signals a transition to a new thought or line of argument.

How are words such as *vital, must,* and *hysteria* meant to strike the reader?

What is the argument put forward in this paragraph? How is the argument supported? Do you find the evidence provided to be compelling? Why or why not?

This paragraph extends the argument made in the previous paragraph.

have suggested instituting a slew of policies that drastically alter the balance between government and the individual. Whether denying the right of a terror suspect to consult with a lawyer or allowing the government greater latitude to spy on its citizens, these measures are designed to make the United States a safer place. That is a worthy goal; and perhaps stricter measures such as these will help accomplish that task.

Building a safer America, however, must not be the only important goal. Many of the proposed suggestions run roughshod over the rights of ordinary people—rights enshrined in the Constitution and held as dear by generations of Americans. These rights are vital to the well-being of America; they must not be tossed aside like pieces of confetti. Yes, it is essential to fight the war on terror. But this battle must be waged without sacrificing the liberties of the American people. By instituting these measures, the United States would be succumbing to hysteria over terrorism—and, in the process, destroying its very soul.

The laws and customs of the United States are based on a strong foundation: respect for individual liberties. The first ten amendments to the U.S. Constitution, collectively known as the Bill of Rights, enumerate many of these—the right to free speech, the freedom to practice religion, the right to bear arms, and more. These rights are clear and sweeping. They do not depend on the whims of judges, legislatures, or presidents. The Sixth Amendment to the Constitution, for example, requires that defendants be given speedy trials; the Fourth Amendment, likewise, guarantees the right of people "to be secure in their persons, houses, papers, or effects." Americans must not sacrifice these basic constitutional rights in their zeal to protect themselves from terrorist attacks.

President George W. Bush and others have argued that the special circumstances of wartime require that these rights be limited. It is true that past presidents have suspended some of these rights during conflict. During the Civil War, for instance, Abraham Lincoln imprisoned some suspected criminals far longer than the law typically allowed. Franklin Roosevelt, fearing that Japanese Americans might be secretly working with Japan during World War II, moved thousands of them into resettlement camps in America's interior. But these historical parallels do not justify further limits on civil rights. On the contrary, Lincoln and Roosevelt were wrong. During the Civil War era, Lincoln was widely criticized for his policies, and Roosevelt's decision to resettle Japanese Americans is recognized today as a national disgrace. Even in cases of great danger, the federal government must not arbitrarily suspend the civil rights of Americans.

What opposing argument is offered here? How does the essay meet this objection?

Those in favor of strict antiterrorism measures claim that ordinary Americans have nothing to fear because the new laws will be used only against terrorists. "There is no evidence of any abuse of Patriot Act provisions," writes former attorney general Edwin Meese III, discussing the impact of a strict antiterror law passed soon after the September 11 hijackings. But it is naive to believe that such abuse will never happen. As government powers increase at the expense of the rights of ordinary citizens, even law-abiding Americans may come under government scrutiny. As the American Civil Liberties Union puts it, laws such as the Patriot Act "increase the chances that innocent Americans will be swept into terrorist investigations by removing traditional checks and balances on law enforcement." This is terrible news for anyone the least bit concerned with the rights of ordinary Americans.

This paragraph introduces a new subtopic. What is the thrust of this argument? Express it in your own words.

This paragraph includes two quotes. Why are there two? What is the purpose of each quote? Why does the order of the quotes matter?

Moreover, plenty of evidence exists to prove that not all terror suspects are terrorists. Since September 11, 2001, the United States has captured and locked up hundreds of suspected terrorists, including several U.S. citizens. Some of these prisoners, to be sure, have strong ties to terror organizations and a history of violence. There is clear proof that they present a danger to the security of the United States. All Americans can applaud the capture of these fanatics and hope they receive a swift and appropriate punishment.

This paragraph and the next discuss the final argument. Why is this argument divided into two paragraphs? What is the function of each?

But other terror suspects present a very different situation. Those imprisoned by the United States on terror charges include any number of people who simply happened to be in the wrong place at the wrong time. In late 2004 and early 2005, for instance, the United States quietly released over 150 prisoners from its detention center at Guantánamo Bay, Cuba. In essence, the government admitted that these people had been detained in error. Some had been at the base for two or even three years, all without access to a lawyer or, in some cases, even knowing the exact nature of the charges against them. To treat innocent people this way is appalling; but such treatment is the natural consequence of strict antiterror legislation.

Terrorists strike at America to destroy its buildings and its people; but there is more than one way to destroy a nation. By limiting constitutional freedoms, by dramatically expanding government powers, those working to implement stricter antiterrorism measures are diminishing America's greatness. If they have their way, America will be much the poorer for it. No one denies that terrorism is a threat; no one argues that law enforcement officials should protect the American people. But government must be careful to keep a balance between public safety and the cherished constitutional rights enjoyed by all Americans. To do otherwise would be unacceptable.

How does the conclusion restate earlier ideas? How does it move the discussion forward?

Write a Conclusion and Complete Your Essay

If you have completed the first three exercises, you now have written four paragraphs of a persuasive essay. The main piece that remains is the conclusion.

Recall that the conclusion to an essay brings the writing to a close. It is your last chance to convince your readers that your argument is logical and important. As a consequence, it is necessary that a conclusion makes your perspective absolutely clear. The conclusion should therefore restate and summarize ideas presented in the previous paragraphs. Most effective conclusions, however, go further than this. Though they probably will not bring in completely new ideas, they usually offer a new way of looking at the evidence, or they may explore the deeper implications of the topic. Briefly review the viewpoints and the model essays once more to find techniques for doing this. The sidebars to the model essays may be especially helpful. Now, write a conclusion for the essay you began earlier.

The steps listed so far—outline, introduction, arguments, and conclusion—represent one way to go about writing a five-paragraph essay. As mentioned earlier, there are others. Some writers prefer to write the body of the essay before fleshing out the introduction; some use graphic organizers, such as diagrams, in place of formal outlines. Whatever system you use, your work is not done when you finish the last paragraph. Now it is time to go back and reread the entire essay to make sure it is clear, organized, and, most of all, convincing. Check spelling, grammar, and other mechanical aspects of your writing; be sure you have appropriate transitions between ideas. Delete unnecessary words, and add information when a topic is unclear. You may have changed your views or your arguments slightly while writing; as you revise, make sure you look back at earlier paragraphs to see if they need to be changed, too. Remember, your overall goal is to do your best work.

Section Three: Supporting Research Material

Facts About Terrorism

Editor's Note: These facts can be used in reports or papers to reinforce or add credibility when making important points or claims.

- In 2004, according to the National Counterterrorism Center, 651 significant terrorist strikes occurred worldwide, causing a total of 9,321 casualties. Americans accounted for just over 1 percent of the casualties. Since 1982, when American government agencies began to count incidents of terrorism, only the year 1987, with 665 recorded attacks, has a higher number of terrorist strikes.
- According to the U.S. Department of State, the government agency responsible for counting terrorist attacks before 2004, 190 significant terrorist attacks occurred in 2003, 198 in 2002, 355 in 2001, and 426 in 2000.
- In most recent years, the region with the greatest number of terrorist attacks and casualties is Asia (excluding the Middle East). Typically, Latin America and the Middle East experience many more terrorist attacks than Africa and Europe, and Oceania and North America have the fewest.
- The word *terrorism* stems from the Reign of Terror, a particularly bloody period of the French Revolution. During 1793 and 1794, thousands of people were executed, some under extremely brutal circumstances.
- *Terrorism* is usually defined as the use of force by people or groups not acting as part of a national army, although some terrorist groups have had close ties to certain national governments.
- As of 2002, according to the U.S. Department of State, Iraq, Cuba, Syria, Sudan, Libya, Iran, and North Korea were considered "state sponsors of terrorism"—that is, nations that support and assist various terrorist organizations.
- Terrorists and terrorist groups may be motivated either by political or religious concerns or a mixture of both.

- Middle Eastern groups active in terrorism recently include al Qaeda, Hamas, Islamic Jihad, and Hizballah, all radical Islamic groups; and Kahane Chai, a radical Israeli organization.
- Non–Middle Eastern terrorist groups of note include the Peruvian group Tupac Amaru, the Irish Republican Army of Northern Ireland, the Liberation Tigers in Sri Lanka, and the Aum Shinrikyo cult in Japan.
- Terrorists rarely call themselves terrorists, preferring instead terms such as *revolutionary, guerrilla,* or *freedom fighter.*
- While most terrorist attacks rely on bombs and other explosives, some terrorist groups have used or tried to acquire chemical and biological agents of mass destruction as well. Some government authorities believe that a widespread release of smallpox germs, for instance, could kill up to three hundred thousand Americans in a short period of time.
- Suicide bombing, in which terrorists strap explosives to their bodies and blow themselves up along with their targets, is a technique originated and used regularly by Hamas and other Islamic terrorist organizations.
- The September 11, 2001, attacks on America rank as the deadliest terrorist attacks in history to date.
- About half of the nearly three thousand people killed in the September 11, 2001, attacks were U.S. citizens.
- President George W. Bush signed the Aviation and Transportation Security Act in November 2001. This act called for fortified cockpit doors aboard passenger aircraft, more rigid screening procedures at airports, explosive-detection systems, more plainclothes sky marshals aboard airplanes, and several similar measures.
- Immediately following the September 11 attacks, all U.S. borders were briefly closed while officials assessed the dangers of terrorists crossing the boundary between the United States and Canada or the United States and Mexico.

- All nineteen of the September 11 hijackers had visas issued by American authorities that allowed them to be in the United States legally.
- Congress approved the Patriot Act in October 2001. This bill gave the government greater powers to gather information on suspected terrorists; for instance, it increased the ability of law enforcement officials to order wiretaps, carry out searches, and access e-mail records.
- Between September 11 and early November 2001, more than one thousand people, most of them noncitizens, had been detained by the U.S. government on suspicion of terrorist activity.
- The Department of Homeland Security, a new Cabinet-level federal office, was approved by Congress in November 2002. It is charged with overseeing federal antiterrorism efforts and coordinating what is done by several different agencies.
- In 2002 President George W. Bush authorized the Central Intelligence Agency to kill terrorist Osama bin Laden and other al Qaeda leaders if they could not be captured. As of July 2005, bin Laden has not been found.
- In July 2004 a bipartisan commission charged with investigating the September 11 attacks issued its final report. Citing many instances of intelligence failures, the report called for sweeping changes in the way the United States gathers and processes information relating to national security.
- Less than 1 percent of the U.S. budget goes to foreign aid. The largest share of foreign aid goes to Israel, the second largest share to Egypt. Most foreign aid goes for economic assistance; some goes for peacekeeping operations or military support.
- Some of the most significant instances of terrorism involving the United States include the following:

  October 23, 1983: Suicide bombers detonate explosives at a U.S. military base in Beirut, Lebanon, killing 241 Marines.

October 7, 1985: Italian cruise ship *Achille Lauro* is hijacked; one American tourist is killed.

December 18, 1985: Airports in Rome and Vienna are bombed; twenty people are killed, including five Americans.

February 26, 1993: Six people are killed and over a thousand are injured during a car bombing of the World Trade Center masterminded by Pakistani terrorist Ramzi Yousef.

April 19, 1995: American antigovernment activists Timothy McVeigh and Terry Nichols explode a truck bomb outside the Alfred P. Murrah Federal Building in Oklahoma City, killing 168.

June 25, 1996: Nineteen American soldiers are killed by a truck bomb detonated by the radical Islamic group Hizballah at a military complex in Dhahran, Saudi Arabia.

August 7, 1998: U.S. embassies in Tanzania and Kenya are destroyed by bombs, killing 224 and injuring about 4,000.

October 12, 2000: The U.S. Navy ship *Cole* is badly damaged by a bomb detonated on a nearby small boat in the Gulf of Aden. Seventeen sailors are killed.

September 11, 2001: Four U.S. passenger aircraft are hijacked by al Qaeda terrorists. Two of the planes are flown into the World Trade Center's Twin Towers, one into the Pentagon. The fourth plane crashes in southwestern Pennsylvania. The death toll approaches three thousand.

October 5, 2001: A worker at a publishing company in Florida dies from anthrax spores sent through the mail, one of several such attacks during this time; the perpetrators have not yet been identified.

May 12, 2003: Suicide bombers kill thirty-four people at a housing compound in Saudi Arabia reserved for Westerners. Eight of the dead are Americans.

Finding and Using Sources of Information

When you write a persuasive essay, it is necessary to find information to support your point of view. You can use sources such as books, magazine articles, newspaper articles, and online articles.

Using Books and Articles

You can find books and articles in a library by using the card catalog or the library's online catalog. If you are not sure how to use these resources, ask a librarian to help you. You can also use a computer to find many magazine articles and other articles written specifically for the Internet.

You are likely to find a lot more information than you can possibly use in your essay, so your first task is to narrow it down to what is likely to be most usable. Look at book and article titles. Look at book chapter titles, and examine the book's index to see if it contains information on the specific topic you want to write about.

For a five-paragraph essay, you do not need a great deal of supporting information, so quickly try to narrow down your materials to a few good books and magazine or Internet articles. You do not need dozens. You might even find that one or two good books or articles contain all the information you need.

You probably do not have time to read an entire book, so find the chapters or sections that relate to your topic, and skim these. When you find useful information, copy it onto a notecard or notebook. You should look for supporting facts, statistics, quotations, and examples.

Evaluate the Source

When you select your supporting information, it is important that you evaluate its source. This is especially important with information you find on the Internet. Because nearly anyone can put information on the Internet, there is as much bad information as good information. Before using Internet information—or any information—try to determine if the source seems to be reliable. Is the author or Internet site sponsored by a legitimate organization? Is it from a government source? Does the author have any special knowledge or training relating to the topic you are looking up? Does the article give any indication of where its information comes from?

Using Your Supporting Information

When you use supporting information from a book, article, interview or other source, there are three important things to remember:

1. Make it clear whether you are using a direct quotation or a paraphrase. If you copy information directly from your source, you are quoting it. You must put quotation marks around the information, and tell where the information comes from. If you put the information in your own words, you are paraphrasing it.

Here is an example of using a quotation:
Author Katrina Rollins is one person who believes that efforts to improve America's transportation have largely been futile. Writes Rollins: "The nation's new and improved airport security is a joke; all the stories about little blue-haired ladies' shoes search for explosives are true. Americans know the hassle and make-work and plastic forks don't add to their safety."[1]

Here is an example of a brief paraphrase of the same passage:
Author Katrina Rollins argues that efforts to improve America's transportation systems have largely been futile. She believes that adjustments to the nation's

---

1. Katrina Rollins, "No Compromises: Why We Are Going to Lose the War on Terror . . . and How We Could Win," *American Enterprise*, January/February 2003, p. 18.

airlines, such as using plastic silverware and randomly searching obviously harmless passengers, have not made America any safer—such changes have only made airport security seem like a waste of time.

2. Use the information fairly. Be careful to use supporting information in the way the author intended it. For example, it is unfair to quote an author as saying, "Nuclear power works" when he or she intended to say, "Nuclear power works *against the people's best interests*." This is called taking information out of context. This is using supporting evidence unfairly.

3. Give credit where credit is due. You must give credit when you use someone else's information, but not every piece of supporting information needs a credit.
    • If the supporting information is general knowledge—that is, it can be found in many sources—you do not have to cite (give credit to) your source.
    • If you directly quote a source, you must give credit.
    • If you paraphrase information from a specific source, you must give credit.

If you do not give credit where you should, you are plagiarizing—or stealing—someone else's work.

Giving Credit
There are a number of ways to give credit. Your teacher will probably want you to do it in one of three ways:
    • Informal: As in the examples in number 1 above, you tell where you got the information in the same place you use it.
    • Informal list: At the end of the article, place an unnumbered list of the sources you used. This tells the reader where, in general, you got your information.

- Formal: Use a footnote, like the first example in number 1 above. (A footnote is generally placed at the end of an article or essay, although it may be located in different places depending on your teacher's requirements.)

Your teacher will tell you exactly how information should be credited in your essay. Generally, the very least information needed is the original author's name and the name of the article or other publication.

Be sure you know exactly what information your teacher requires before you start looking for your supporting information so that you know what information to include with your notes.

Sample Essay Topics

The Threat of Terrorism
The War on Terror Has Been Successful
The War on Terror Has Been a Failure
A War on Terror Is Futile
The War on Terror Intimidates Terrorists
It Is Too Early to Determine the Outcome of the War on Terror
Americans Have the Right to Question the War on Terror
The War on Terror Has Made America Safer from Terrorism
The War on Terror Has Not Made America Safer from Terrorism
The Threat of Terrorism Has Been Exaggerated
Weapons of Mass Destruction Pose a Serious Threat
Weapons of Mass Destruction Are Unlikely to Be Used by Terrorists

The Causes of Terrorism
Despair and Poverty Cause Terrorism
Despair and Poverty Do Not Cause Terrorism
Religious Fanaticism Causes Terrorism
Religious Fanaticism Does Not Always Cause Terrorism
The Promise of an Afterlife Motivates Terrorists
America's Foreign Policy Causes Terrorism

Preventing Terrorism
Expanding Government Powers Can Prevent Terrorism
Expanding Government Powers Cannot Prevent Terrorism
Expanded Government Powers Violate Civil Liberties
Military Action Should Be Used to Prevent Terrorism
Military Action Should Not Be Used to Prevent Terrorism
Forming Global Alliances Is the Best Way to Fight Terrorism
Racial Profiling Is Necessary to Prevent Terrorism
Racial Profiling Is Unnecessary and Harmful

Organizations to Contact

American Civil Liberties Union (ACLU)
125 Broad St., 18th Floor, New York, NY 10014
(212) 549-2500 • Web site: www.aclu.org

The ACLU is a national organization dedicated to the preservation of civil rights guaranteed by the U. S. Constitution. The organization argues that measures to protect national security, including from terrorist attacks, must not infringe upon these basic liberties.

Cato Institute
1000 Massachusetts Ave. NW, Washington, DC 20001
(202) 842-0200 • Web site: www.cato.org

Dedicated to preserving individual liberties and limiting the power of government, Cato Institute issues policy papers, articles, and other information related to the problem of terrorism.

Center for Defense Information
1779 Massachusetts Ave. NW, Washington, DC 20036
(202) 332-0600 • Web site: www.cdi.org

Founded in 1972, the Center for Defense Information studies security issues and advocates for changes in the current American military strategy. It works toward such goals as international cooperation and reform of the military establishment.

Center for Immigration Studies
1522 K St. NW, Suite 820, Washington, DC 20005
(202) 466-8185 • Web site: www.cis.org

Founded in 1985, the Center for Immigration Studies focuses on the impact of immigration on American society. Some of its many publications and policy papers discuss the question of terrorism as it relates to immigration policy.

Council on American-Islamic Relations

453 New Jersey Ave. SE, Washington, DC 20003

(202) 488-8787• Web site: www.cair-net.org

The Council on American-Islamic Relations presents an Islamic perspective on issues of public interest. It seeks to correct misconceptions of Muslims and the Islamic faith.

Council on Foreign Relations

58 E. Sixty-eighth St., New York, NY 10021

(212) 434-9400 •Web site: www.cfr.org

This nonpartisan organization seeks to create a better understanding of the world and the foreign policy choices faced by different nations, particularly the United States. It offers a valuable question-and-answer section on terrorism as part of its Web site.

Department of Homeland Security (DHS)

Washington, DC 20528

Web site: www.dhs.gov/dhspublic

The Department of Homeland Security was created shortly after the attacks of September 11, 2001. The role of the DHS is to prevent terrorist attacks against Americans and to respond quickly and effectively to attacks that may nevertheless occur.

Global Exchange

2017 Mission, #303, San Francisco, CA 94110

(415) 255-7296 • fax: (415) 255-7498

Web site: www.globalexchange.org

Global Exchange is a human rights organization that aims to expose economic and political injustice. It believes the best solution to such injustices is education, activism, and a noninterventionist U.S. foreign policy, and it opposes military retaliation in response to terrorist attacks.

International Policy Institute for Counter-Terrorism (ICT)

PO Box 167, Herzlia, 46150, Israel• 972-9-9527277
fax: 972-9-9513073 • e-mail: info@ict.org.il
Web site: www.ict.org.il

ICT is a research institute that develops public policy solutions to international terrorism. Its Web site is a comprehensive resource on terrorism and counterterrorism, including an extensive database on terrorist organizations.

U. S. Department of State, Counterterrorism Office

2201 C St. NW, Washington, DC 20520
(202) 647-4000 • Web site: www.state.gov/s/ct

This government office develops and carries out policies and strategies related to containing and defeating terrorism. It offers news articles, press releases, and speeches by government officials through its Web site.

Terrorism Research Center

(877) 635-0816 • Web site: www.terrorism.com

The goal of the Terrorism Research Center is to inform the public on terrorism and information warfare. The site features profiles of terrorist organizations, essays and analyses, and links to other terrorism-related documents and resources.

Bibliography

Books

Graham Allison, *Nuclear Terrorism: The Ultimate Preventable Catastrophe.* New York: Times Books, 2004.

Richard Clarke, *Against All Enemies: Inside America's War on Terror.* New York: Free Press, 2004.

Gavin de Becker, *Fear Less.* Boston: Little, Brown, 2002.

Stephen Flynn, *America the Vulnerable.* New York: Harper-Collins, 2004.

David Frum and Richard Perle, *An End to Evil: How to Win the War on Terror.* New York: Random House, 2003.

Bill Gertz, *Treachery: How America's Friends and Foes Are Secretly Arming Our Enemies.* New York: Crown, 2004.

Bob Graham and Jeff Nussbaum, *Intelligence Matters: The CIA, the FBI, Saudi Arabia, and the Failure of America's War on Terror.* New York: Random House, 2004.

Michelle Malkin, *In Defense of Internment: The Case for "Racial Profiling" in World War II and the War on Terror.* Washington, DC: Regnery, 2004.

Terry McDermott, *Perfect Soldiers: The Hijackers: Who They Were, Why They Did It.* New York: HarperCollins, 2005.

Jonathan Randal, *Osama: The Making of a Terrorist.* New York: Knopf, 2004.

Marcus Ranum, *The Myth of Homeland Security.* Hoboken, NJ: John Wiley and Sons, 2003.

Bruce Schneier, *Beyond Fear: Thinking Sensibly About Security in an Uncertain World.* New York: Copernicus, 2003.

Bob Woodward, *Bush at War.* New York: Simon & Schuster, 2002.

Periodicals

Atlanta Journal-Constitution, "Civil Liberties Need Protective Custody," March 27, 2005.

Russ Feingold, "U.S. Losing the Race to Engage Muslims," *Christian Science Monitor,* February 7, 2005.

Douglas J. Feith, "Freedom, Safety, and Sovereignty," www.pentagon.gov, February 17, 2005.

Georgie Anne Geyer, "Iraq War Is Spawning Terrorism, Anti-Americanism in Islamic World," *Columbus Dispatch,* December 7, 2003.

Bob Herbert, "It's Called Torture," *New York Times,* February 28, 2005.

Jeff Jacoby, "Why Not Torture Terrorists?" www.town hall.com, March 21, 2005.

Heather MacDonald, "Too Nice for Our Own Good," *Wall Street Journal,* January 6, 2005.

Michelle Malkin, "Racial Profiling: A Matter of Survival," *USA Today,* August 17, 2004.

Salam Al-Marayati, "Guilty of 'Flying While Muslim'?" *Los Angeles Times,* December 11, 2004.

J.F.O. McAllister, "You Can't Kill Them All: Pre-Emptive Strikes Against Terror Will Win Some Battles but Lose the War," *Time International,* August 4, 2003.

Edwin Meese III, "Patriot Act's Bum Rap," *Washington Times,* July 8, 2004.

George Melloan, "Making Muslims Part of the Solution," *Wall Street Journal,* March 29, 2005.

Leonard Pitts, "Moral Failure 'Happening All Over Again,'" *Chicago Tribune,* November 16, 2004.

Pittsburgh Post-Gazette, "Security First: Slow the Rush to Arm American Pilots," August 29, 2003.

Robert W. Poole Jr. and Jim Harper, "Transportation Security Aggravation," *Reason,* March 2005.

Thomas J. Raleigh, "U.S. Must Regain Moral Ascendancy," *Christian Science Monitor,* February 1, 2005.

Joan Ryan, "Not All Citizens Have Rights," *San Francisco Chronicle,* January 13, 2005.

St. Louis Post-Dispatch, "Liberty vs. Security," December 30, 2003.

Paul Shrivastava, "We Don't Understand Terrorism," *Patriot News* (Harrisburg, PA), October 25, 2004.

Micah L. Sifry and Nancy Watzman, "Security for Sale," *Nation,* October 4, 2004.

Jack Spencer and Ha Nguyen, "Is U.S. Safer Since September 11 Attacks?" *Heritage Foundation Policy Research and Analysis,* September 15, 2003.

Stuart Taylor Jr., "Distorting the Law and Facts in the Torture Debate," *National Journal,* January 15, 2005.

Paul Wolfowitz, "Support Our Troops," *Wall Street Journal,* September 2, 2003.

Index

Abdullah, Ali, 31
Abu Ghraib prison, 57
Afghanistan, 11, 17
  interrogations in,
    53–54
Alter, Jonathan, 60
American Civil Liberties
  Union (ACLU), 87
America the Vulnerable
  (Flynn), 38
Ansar-al-Islam (radical
  group), 25
anthrax attacks, 49
antiterrorism measures,
  17–18
  versus civil liberties,
    82–83, 86–88
Asharq Al-Awsat (news-
  paper), 29
Atta, Muhammad, 76

Beslan (Russia) attack,
  28, 30
bin Laden, Osama, 11,
  76
Bratton, William, 43
Bush, George W., 20, 21,
  54, 86
  on Middle East, 20

on reasons for Iraq
  invasion, 11–12

Central Intelligence
  Agency (CIA), secret
  prisons of, 27
Chechnya, 31
civil rights, versus
  antiterrorism measures,
  82–83, 86–87
Convention Against
  Torture and Other
  Cruel, Inhuman, or
  Degrading Treatment or
  Punishment, 58–59

de Becker, Gavin, 38, 45
Department of
  Homeland Security, 12

Fear Less (de Becker), 45
Feith, Douglas J., 16
Flynn, Stephen, 38, 77

Geneva Conventions, 54,
  59

Picture Credits

About the Editor

Stephen Currie is the author of more than forty books for young adults. He has written on a wide variety of topics, including terrorist groups, the Holocaust, and slavery. He has also written numerous magazine articles, book reviews, and educational materials. He lives in New York State with his wife and children.